FAITH DEVELOPMENT
OF
GOD'S PEOPLE

Genesis through Revelation

by Dr. J. A. Phillips

FAITH DEVELOPMENT OF GOD'S PEOPLE
Genesis through Revelation

Cover layout in collaboration with
Jeff Thorne

ISBN 0-9710031-3-0

Web Site: http://www.GloryQuests.com

FAITH DEVELOPMENT
OF GOD'S PEOPLE
Genesis Through Revelation

Faith Development pertains to the developmental capacity for faith as meaning-making. As such, it provides identity and is considered a basic stage developmental theory in the area of human development. It also leads to maturity.

The growth and development of the nation of Israel and the Church, as set forth in Scripture, are analyzed from a faith development perspective. The benefits of such a study are the following:

1. Understanding of the correspondence and unity between the Old and New Testaments.

2. Insight into the purpose of the Law given in the Old Testament and in the ceremonial rituals.

3. A perspective of God's actions throughout history and today.

4. A better understanding of God and human nature.

5. A view of the revealed end from the beginning and insight into the events in between.

6. Clarification of the Judeo-Christian connection.

7. A comprehension of faith as meaning-making from a scriptural perspective.

The author, **Dr. J. A. Phillips**, a licensed minister, has a Ph.D. in Theology from Walden University and an M.A. in Bible and Theology from Simpson University. Currently, Dr. Phillips is a professor of Bible and Theology, Author, and Speaker.

*"'I will be your father,
and you shall be my sons and daughters,'
says the Lord Almighty."*

2 Corinthians 6:18—NRSV

*". . . I took them by the hand
to lead them . . . "*

Hebrews 8:9—NRSV

TABLE OF CONTENTS

LIST OF ILLUSTRATIONS

INTRODUCTION

I

God's people, with respect to the development of the nation of Israel and the Church, have some noted similarities with human development, especially in the areas of faith development, cognitive development, and psychosocial development. Stages in human development seem to correspond to the development of Israel and the Church as recorded in Scripture. It is an interesting comparison, human development with a nation and the Church. This work will attempt to set forth corresponding similarities of relationship in growth. The nation of Israel and the Church, as set forth in Scripture, will be considered from a human developmental perspective, emphasizing their capacity for faith and noting identity and maturity which also are factors of faith development.

A work of this nature, which analyzes development, can help one to understand the correspondence and unity between the Old and New Testaments. It can open up insight into the purpose of the law given in the Old Testament and in the ceremonial rituals. It can help one gain a perspective of what God was doing then and now. It can help one gain a better understanding of God and human nature. It can help one see the revealed end from the beginning and gain insight into the events in between. It can clarify the Judeo-Christian connection. And it can help in understanding faith as meaning-making from a scriptural perspective.

It is not too far-fetched to analyze the development of "God's people" using a human developmental concept since throughout Scripture the metaphor of God being a father and the nation of Israel being children occurs.[1] Considering this metaphor, it appears that the revelation given by God to Israel in the early stages of Israel's history was as from a father to children who were developing. At first, the revelation was simple, uncomplicated, and foundational. Also, it was symbolic for children who needed to picture abstract concepts through the tangible. Gradually, God's revelation became more detailed and complex. Israel is seen to respond to the revelation of God as children do to the instruction of their parents and others in authority. God is noted to be very patient with them, as a loving father to his children.

<u>Metaphorical Sonship</u>

The parent-child relationship of Israel to God is actually portrayed as that of a son to a father. Indeed, Israel is referred to as God's firstborn son, as Scripture records, "Thus says the LORD: 'Israel is My son, My firstborn'" (Exodus 4:22, NKJV); and, "I am a Father to Israel, And Ephraim [a term often used for Israel] is My firstborn" (Jeremiah 31:9, NKJV). In this father-son relationship, God indicates that He disciplines His people as a father does a son. Deuteronomy 8:5 states, "Know then in your heart that as a parent disciplines a child so the LORD your God disciplines you [referring to Israel]" (NIV). A similar statement is found in Proverbs 3:11-12, "My child, do not despise the LORD's discipline or be weary of his reproof, for the LORD reproves the one he loves, as a father the son in whom he delights" (NRSV). And with respect to the Church, the same relationship is communicated in Hebrews 12:5-11 (NIV):

You have forgotten that word of encouragement
that addresses you as sons: "My son, do not make light

---

[1]See Isaiah 9:6; Jeremiah 3:21-22; 50:4; Ezekiel 44:15; Hosea 3:5; 4:1; Amos 4:5.

of the Lord's discipline, and do not lose heart when he rebukes you, because the Lord disciplines those he loves, and he punishes everyone he accepts as a son." Endure hardship as discipline; God is treating you as sons. For what son is not disciplined by his father? If you are not disciplined (and everyone undergoes discipline), then you are illegitimate children and not true sons. Moreover, we have all had human fathers who disciplined us and we respected them for it. How much more should we submit to the Father of our spirits and live! Our fathers disciplined us for a little while as they thought best; but God disciplines us for our good, that we may share in his holiness. No discipline seems pleasant at the time, but painful. Later on, however, it produces a harvest of righteousness and peace for those who have been trained by it.

Being a firstborn son was not to be taken lightly. Although privileges were associated in the relationship, there also were concomitant responsibilities. Privileges involved a special paternal blessing and treatment, extra respect by others, a double portion of the inheritance (two portions compared with one portion each which the other sons received), and an honored place during meals. Responsibilities included leadership of the family after the father's death, which involved caring for the mother and unmarried sisters as well as spiritual headship that constituted priestly duties for the family during the patriarchal time frame. Technically, the firstborn son belonged to God (Ex. 13:2), thus the spiritual headship. However, after the institution of the Levitical priesthood, parents were required to pay a redemption price to the priest for their firstborn son (Numbers 3:11-13, 45; 18:16).[2]

---

[2]Geoffrey W. Bromiley, gen. ed. The International Standard Bible Encyclopedia, fully revised, vol. 2 (Grand Rapids, MI: William B. Eerdmans Publishing Company, 1982), s.v. "First-Born; Firstling," by T. Lewis; Merrill C. Tenney, gen. ed. The Zondervan Pictorial Encyclopedia of the Bible, vol. 2 (Grand Rapids, MI: Zondervan Publishing Company, 1976), s.v. "First-Born," by J. E.

In the above description, it is evident that the firstborn son carried the idea of priority and supremacy. However, it also connoted preeminence. The firstborn son was considered the prominent one to care for his family and to lead them properly in spiritual guidance and representation. Their welfare, both materially and spiritually, was to be his concern and responsibility.

As the firstborn son of God, Israel was given special blessings but also was given responsibility. And the blessings would not come without fulfillment of responsibility. The two were connected. This is discussed further under the topic of Meaning Making in connection with the discussion of the purpose for Israel as God's firstborn son.

Meaning Making

Israel was to have its own unique meaning in God's creation. God had a purpose in considering Israel as His firstborn son, and in fulfillment of His purpose, Israel would be blessed. The purpose was three-fold and is found in Exodus 19:5-6 (NKJV), "If you will indeed obey My voice and keep My covenant, then you shall be a special treasure to Me above all people; for all the earth is Mine. And you shall be to Me a kingdom of priests and a holy nation." Israel, as firstborn son, was to be a special treasure, a kingdom of priests, and a holy nation. Actually, Israel was to obey God and in so doing would be a holy nation. As a holy nation to God, Israel would be His special treasure. And as God's special treasure, Israel would fulfill special responsibility, being a kingdom of priests.[3] In other words, Israel would

---

Rosscup; George Arthur Buttrick, dict. ed. <u>The Interpreter's Dictionary of the Bible</u>, vol. 2 (Nashville: Abingdon Press, 1962), s.v. "First-Born," by V. H. Kooy; J. D. Douglas, org. ed. <u>New Bible Dictionary</u>, 2nd ed. (Wheaton: Tyndale House Publishers, Inc., 1982), s.v. "First-Born," by M. J. Selman; Herbert Lockyer, Sr., gen. ed. <u>Nelson's Illustrated Bible Dictionary</u> (Nashville: Thomas Nelson Publishers, 1986), s.v. "Firstborn."

[3] James Fowler also recognized that Israel was "a community fit to be priests to other nations." James W. Fowler, <u>Stages of Faith: The Psychology of Human Development and the Quest for Meaning</u> (San Francisco: HarperColins, Publishers, 1981), 206.

fulfill the spiritual responsibility as God's firstborn with respect to other nations.

Technically, priests were considered to be mediators between humanity and God, leaders in worship, teachers of God's revelation and enforcers of it. But they could not teach and represent others in approach to the holy God if they were not in right standing with God and holy or considered cleansed themselves. However, if they were obedient and, thus, considered holy, they would be blessed by God as His special treasure. Blessings involved protection from enemies, abundant crops, good health, growth in numbers of Israelites, and God's presence among them (Exodus 15:26; Leviticus 26). As they were blessed, Israel was to fulfill priestly responsibility by being a witness to the surrounding nations of the blessings of God; they were to lead the nations to their God because they were to be in right standing with Him and consequently be blessed. Thus, they were to be mediators between other nations and God.

The same purpose for Israel is seen for the Church as noted in 1 Peter 2:9-10 (NIV), "You are a chosen people, a royal priesthood, a holy nation, a people belonging to God, that you may declare the praises of him who called you out of darkness into his wonderful light." The Church also was to be a witness for God in priestly ministry to others, living in fellowship with Him as a people in right standing and cleansed or holy.

Thus, the purpose for Israel and the Church was the same. Israel, as God's firstborn son, was to draw other nations unto Him. This purpose was to give Israel meaning for life and also identity. Israel was not to be like the heathen, but was to be separate and holy and blessed. Thus, others would want to be blessed also and would desire to come to the source of blessing, Israel's God. As the firstborn son, then, Israel would fulfill spiritual responsibility, leading and guiding others to God, revealing God's revelation to the world. Being the firstborn son was to give Israel meaning, purpose, usefulness, and identity. Later, the Church was to have the same meaning, purpose, usefulness, and identity.

But first Israel was to be prepared and developed for meaning making. It was not automatic. And later the Church also was to develop. This development can be viewed against the backdrop of human and faith developmental stages. Thus, before entering into a discussion of Israel and the Church, the topics of human and faith development are presented for clarification of understanding as a foundation for its application to Israel and the Church.

PART I

HUMAN DEVELOPMENT

BACKGROUND

II

Human development is a fairly recent and complicated study.[4] It is more intricate than the study of physical and biological laws of nature which have patterns which can be reliably predicted for the most part. Many variables, seen and unseen, affect human development which contribute toward the difficulty of understanding, influencing, and predicting human behavior which results from human development. However, it is with the desire to help humanity with its behavioral problems that this study has become prominent in this day. The idea is that as personal development or growth can be influenced for the better, societal growth will be positively influenced, the world will be a better place to live, and individuals will be happier.

Determining what is beneficial growth as compared to adverse growth may be a matter of opinion. However, the proposal of this paper is that beneficial growth leads to maturity while adverse growth leads to immaturity. It is proposed herein that maturity is the state of being wherein one has reached a balanced view of self and others, with actions

---

[4]It basically appeared in the philosophy of Georg Hegel in the nineteenth century and soon influenced Karl Marx and, as a result, others. However, traces of the idea of human development can be seen in the writings of the ancient Grecian philosopher Heraclitus "who likened life to a moving stream, always changing, never the same." Louis Breger, <u>From Instinct to Identity: The Development of Personality</u> (Englewood Cliffs, NJ: Prentice-Hall, Inc., 1974), 2.

reflecting concern for and interest in what is best for the welfare of others as well as society as a whole, without neglecting care of self.

In the process of development the dichotomous struggle is seen between self-centeredness and self-giving-ness. When a person is born, that person, of necessity, is self-centered, concerned about his or her own needs and not able to comprehend the needs of others. Healthy growth occurs as one becomes aware of one's own needs and then can perceive the needs of others and become concerned for them also. The process of development seems to fluctuate between the two, concern for self and others, in a cycle of changing and varying focus. Maturity would be considered a stabilized state in which one has reached a healthy perspective of self and desires to live a life in loving service for the benefit of others and society which is seen in positive, consistent action.

In growth and development, a person's actions reflect the state of maturity or lack thereof. And in the process, one begins to take on an identity, an individuality, which is seen in qualities which make each person similar to others yet uniquely different at the same time. Along this line of thinking, it has been stated that "each person is unique; and yet people are different in predictably similar ways."[5] Technically, identity is defined as "the collective aspect of the set of characteristics by which a thing is definitely recognizable or known; the set of behavioral or personal characteristics by which an individual is recognizable as a member of a group; the quality or condition of being the same as something else; the distinct personality of an individual regarded as a persisting entity; individuality."[6] In essence, identity has to do with how a person is distinguished and known. It involves individuality which reflects personality, the uniqueness of individual persons. Thus, personality consists of "the totality of qualities and traits, as of character or behavior, that are peculiar to an individual person; a person as the embodiment

---

[5] David O. Yates, <u>What the Bible Says About Your Personality</u> (San Francisco: Harper & Row, Publishers), 3.

[6] <u>American Heritage Dictionary</u>, 1986 ed., s.v. "Identity."

of distinctive traits of mind and behavior . . . the pattern of collective character, behavioral, temperamental, emotional, and mental traits of an individual."[7] The qualities which make up personality involve growth areas which are influenced in the process of development and provide the uniqueness of individuality and identity.

In ancient biblical times (and occasionally in the present), a person's identity was often reflected or was hoped to be reflected in the meaning of his or her given name. Often a name given to a baby later was reflected in that person's adult characteristics.[8] The name seemed to be an influence in development, knowingly or unknowingly, a prophetic description of one's ultimate nature. It was not just a means to distinguish one person from another or to use in appellation. "The people of the Bible were very conscious of the meaning of names. They believed there was a vital connection between the name and the person it identified. A name somehow represented the nature of the person."[9] Although there were exceptions, "there is no question but that there is, throughout, a conceptual background which was often given full play in the conferring of a name and which, even if it seemed to have no part (or none that we know) in the original naming yet in later life asserted its claim on the person concerned."[10] This idea may not be limited to antiquity. In naming our first-born child and son, Roger Barry, my husband and I chose family names; Roger was from my husband's brother and Barry was from my father. Later we learned the meaning of these two names and had to laugh because they were quite descriptive of his personality. Roger means "famous spear" with the idea

---

[7] Ibid., s.v. "Personality."

[8] For instance, David means "beloved" or "loved," and God called him "a man after my own heart" (Acts 13:22); Solomon means "peace" or "peaceful," and he had peace virtually during his entire reign over all of Israel; while Nehemiah means "Yahweh Comforts," and he comforted the Jews who had returned from exile, helping and encouraging them to rebuild the wall around Jerusalem and to rebuild their city.

[9] Nelson's Illustrated Bible Dictionary, 1986 ed., s.v. "Name."

[10] New Bible Dictionary: Second Edition, 1982, s.v. "Name."

of warrior and Barry means "spear; hence, straightforward."[11] Unintentionally, we had doubled up on the meaning. In actuality, Roger is very goal oriented, pointing toward the mark he desires to obtain, allowing nothing to distract him in his pursuit, and he is very straightforward. He has time for fun, however, but plans it into his schedule along with family and work. Whatever he does, he performs it with all his might, going straight for the goal before him, just as does a properly guided spear in flight.

Many factors influence identity and maturity. However, when one begins to find meaning and purpose for life, identity and maturity are enhanced. In fact, meaning and purpose are critical in development and well-being. "No man can be happy unless he feels his life in some way important."[12] If there is no reason for being and one's life cannot contribute to anything, all is futile. This futility is described in Ingmar Bergman's film, *The Seventh Seal.* The following is a brief conversation therein about wanting to get rid of God and yet wanting him at the same time and in so doing seeking purpose and meaning:

Knight: Why can't I kill God within me? Why does he live on in this painful and humiliating way, even though I curse him and want to tear him out of my heart? Why, in spite of everything, is he a baffling reality that I can't shake off? Do you hear me?

Death: Yes, I hear you.

Knight: I want knowledge, not faith, not suppositions, but knowledge. I want God to stretch out his hand toward me, reveal himself, speak to me.

Death: But he remains silent.

Knight: I call out to him in the dark, but no one seems to be there.

---

[11]The Reader's Digest Great Encyclopedic Dictionary, 1975 ed. s.v. "Masculine Names: Roger, Barry."

[12]Bertrand Russell, quoted in The Reader's Digest Great Encyclopedia, s.v. "A Dictionary of Quotations: Self-esteem."

Death: Perhaps no one is there.

Knight: Then life is an outrageous horror. No one can live in the face of death knowing that all is nothingness.[13]

Realizing meaning to life and one's place therein makes a world of difference in one's perspective of life and identity. In actuality, one becomes purposeful and significant, not just for self but for meaningful service. One becomes an important part of society, providing a unique contribution to the whole in such a way that only that unique person is able to do. It is much like the various parts of the human body, each of which is vitally important and, though unique, contributes to the proper function of the whole. If one part is not functioning, the whole body suffers. Yet if each functions properly, the body becomes whole and effective.[14]

When a person realizes his or her own uniqueness and how he or she can contribute meaningfully to the wholeness of society, one's identity is revealed in the resultant actions

---

[13]William L. Lane, <u>Hebrews: A Call to Commitment</u> (Peabody, MA: Hendrickson Publishers, 1985), 30.

[14]Scripture comments upon this concept and the uniqueness of each part in 1 Corinthians 12:14-26 (NIV) which deals with the members of the body being organically, cooperatively and sympathetically related:

Now the body is not made up of one part but of many. If the foot should say, "Because I am not a hand, I do not belong to the body," it would not for that reason cease to be part of the body. And if the ear should say, "Because I am not an eye, I do not belong to the body," it would not for that reason cease to be part of the body. If the whole body were an eye, where would the sense of hearing be? If the whole body were an ear, where would the sense of smell be? But in fact God has arranged the parts in the body, every one of them, just as he wanted them to be. If they were all one part, where would the body be? As it is, there are many parts, but one body. The eye cannot say to the hand, "I don't need you!" And the head cannot say to the feet, "I don't need you!" On the contrary, those parts of the body that seem to be weaker are indispensable, and the parts that we think are less honorable we treat with special honor. And the parts that are unpresentable are treated with special modesty, while our presentable parts need no special treatment. But God has combined the members of the body and has given greater honor to the parts that lacked it, so that there should be no division in the body, but that its parts should have equal concern for each other. If one part suffers, every part suffers with it; if one part is honored, every part rejoices with it.

and maturity develops. The study of human development considers this process and can be vitally important in providing keys toward its healthy development.

Human development involves growth in a number of areas which influence identity and maturity. These areas can be placed in six categories: physical, emotional, mental, social, moral and spiritual.[15] No one person grows completely like another person in these areas; the pace, extent, and synchronization vary as do results. This is due to the infinite influences which cause development and growth. The many interdependent and interactive influences come from one's genetic makeup, one's varied and constantly changing environment, and one's own developing behavioral pattern and responses. Plus, a person's past, present and perspective of the future are contributors to diverse and varied growth development. This diversification in growth, then, provides uniqueness and thus identity. Although one often becomes the result of these influences, one is not necessarily at the mercy of them; if desired some can be overcome, though not undone. They can be used positively, whether good or bad originally, in what one becomes. One does make choices, but "life is the art of drawing without an eraser."[16] The individual is the artist, continually making choices, choosing the direction of the brush and the paint to formulate the design. When mistakes or problems occur, however, they cannot be undone but can be turned around for good if the artist is so willing.[17]

---

[15]It is interesting from a Christian perspective that humanity is considered to reflect the image of God (Genesis 1:26-27) in the last five of the growth areas: emotional, mental, social, moral, and spiritual. These lead to identity and personality, another reflection of God in the Christian view.

[16]John Christian, quoted in The Reader's Digest Great Encyclopedic Dictionary, s.v. "A Dictionary of Quotations: Life."

[17]In the Scripture this concept is set forth in the story of Joseph's brothers who intended to harm him, but God is stated to have turned what they did around for good in order to save many lives. In other words, though the brothers tried to get rid of Joseph because of their jealousy with respect to their father's treatment of him, God prepared the way for provision during the future famine by allowing Joseph to go to Egypt as a forerunner for the family, having him learn Egyptian ways as a slave, putting him in prison so the Pharaoh could hear about him, and then elevating him as second in command of all of Egypt with administrative ability to prepare for the coming famine. Joseph had the choice of

In studying human development with respect to identity and maturity, life stages and transitions in this development are considered as well as the influences and processes. A variety of theories have been proposed to account for these stages and development. Some of the theories are similar and develop from or expand upon previous theories, while others differ significantly. However, all have the intent of contributing toward further understanding of behavior and how it can be guided and enhanced for individual betterment as well as the betterment of society as a whole.

---

becoming bitter during his time of hardship as a slave and then as a prisoner or of trusting God to place him where he wanted him for meaningful purpose. Joseph chose the latter and therefore could forgive his brothers and help his family in the long run. His forgiving comment sums up the turning around of wrong intentions for good: "You intended to harm me, but God intended it for good to accomplish what is now being done, the saving of many lives" (Genesis 50:20-NIV).

LIFE STAGE THEORIES

III

As indicated above, human development or growth occurs in six areas or categories: physical, emotional, mental, social, moral, and spiritual. Although a person's physical body begins to grow from birth, it reaches a plateau usually in adulthood and then begins to decline. Normally this physical growth can be charted in stages of development within predictable patterns. However, other areas of human development do not necessarily decline and may continue to develop throughout the life span. Some theorists believe that growth in these other areas fits patterned, sequential stages of development, while others maintain that development is a process and that "there is no single specific route that development must or should take," that it is "potentially multidirectional" occurring "on a number of different fronts."[18]

Whether development is a process or sequential, however, the study of human development should not just be considered the study of "change over time . . . from conception to death"[19] or whatever happens to and in an individual, since this would afford no opportunity to provide developmental

---

[18]Leonie Sugarman, <u>Life-Span Development: Concepts, Theories and Interventions</u> (New York: Methuen & Co., 1986), 2.

[19]Richard Ripple, Robert F. Biehler, and Gail A. Jaquish, <u>Human Development</u> (Boston: Houghton Mifflin Company, 1982), 7.

guidelines for help toward a developmental goal. But "the construct of development centres on some notion of improvement. Changes in amount and in quality are evaluated against some implicit or explicit opinion as to what constitutes the 'good' or the 'ideal.'"[20] Thus, development is compared with an ultimate or desired state or ideal in various areas. Some would call it unattainable perfection, but a more encouraging term would be maturity, the state or quality of being "completely developed or grown"; "highly developed or advanced in intellect, moral qualities, outlook, etc."; "fully or thoroughly developed, perfected, detailed."[21] According to the proposal herein, maturity is "the state of being wherein one has reached a balanced view of self and others, with actions reflecting concern for and interest in what is best for the welfare of others as well as society as a whole, without neglecting care of self."[22] Maslow, in his self-esteem and self-actualization concepts describes the goal of development similarly: "Satisfaction of the self-esteem need leads to feelings of self-confidence, worth, strength, capability, and adequacy, of being useful and necessary in the world"; and self-actualization is considered to be the pinnacle of development with "the full use and exploitation of talents, capacities, potentialities, etc."[23] When a person has developed to a healthy view of self, then that person is free to make his or her abilities available and useful for others. This is maturity.

Maturity of development should affect all six areas of human development, physical, emotional, mental, social, moral, and spiritual, in order for a person to be considered mature and fully developed and fully purposeful. However, one definitely can be significant in the process of development without attaining full maturity. Very few do attain this state,

---

[20]Leonie Sugarman, <u>Life-Span Development: Concepts, Theories and Interventions</u>, 28.

[21]<u>The Reader's Digest Great Encyclopedic Dictionary</u>, s.v. "Mature."

[22]See pages 1-2.

[23]A. H. Maslow, <u>Motivation and Personality</u>, 2nd ed. (New York: Van Nostrand Reinhold, 1968), 45, 150; quoted in Leonie Sugarman, <u>Life-Span Development: Concepts, Theories and Interventions</u>, 30, 31.

but it is an ideal toward which humanity should strive in order to fulfill its full potential.

Life Stages

Some theorists consider that human "development is better thought of as a process than as a state," since they believe development takes no specific, patterned form, order or sequence but can occur in a variety of ways.[24] It is true that there is variety in development, but most development does occur in sequential patterns which are foundational for further development, and these patterns are observable. For instance, learning readiness usually is necessary before a child begins to read. The child must be able to recognize shapes and be able to follow a line of words going from one direction to another (such as left to right on a page as in English writing), then the child must be able to recognize the shape of letters and then to distinguish words and understand their meaning. The same readiness must be developed for a child involved in an athletic game of catch. Motor skills must be developed before the child can play; hand and eye coordination must be such that the child can throw a ball to a designated location and visually follow the path of a thrown ball back and place his or her hands in the appropriate position to catch the ball. Scripture also comments on sequential learning, "Whom will he teach knowledge, and to whom will he explain the message? Those who are weaned from milk, those taken from the breast? For it is precept upon precept, precept upon precept, line upon line, line upon line, here a little, there a little" (Isaiah 28:10-NRSV); and to the Hebrews the comment is made: "For though by this time you ought to be teachers, you need someone to teach you again the basic elements of the oracles of God. You need milk, not solid food; for everyone who lives on milk, being still an infant, is unskilled in the word of righteousness. But solid food is for the mature, for those

---

[24]Leonie Sugarman, Life-Span Development: Concepts, Theories and Interventions, 29.

whose faculties have been trained by practice to distinguish good from evil" (Hebrews 5:12-14).

Sequential human development patterns often can be observed at certain ages of life. Therefore, the idea of life stages of development has been proposed by many in order to evaluate progress at various periods of life. It is acknowledged that these stages are general with latitude of variation. In fact, theorists, themselves, vary on what is normal at what age, but the ages are usually similar and provide a basis for analysis. Erikson has set forth eight life stage ages from his perspective of personality development. His stage ages will be used as a frame of reference from which to evaluate various perspectives of development. His stage ages and the five life stages which will be discussed herein all are charted on Figure 1. Although Erikson did not designate actual ages for every stage and the ages assigned to his categories by several theorists vary, those ages listed on Figure 1 are general and help in visualizing the groups of ages as the life-stage development theories relate to them.[25]

Freud - Psychosexual

Sigmund Freud was born May 6, 1856, in Freiberg, Moravia, which is now part of Czechoslovakia, but lived most of his life in Austria until the Nazi occupation when he moved in 1938 to England where he died on September 23, 1939. He studied for a career in medical research, being trained as a physician. His first work was in the area of developmental-neurological research pertaining to brain damage which led to interest in psychology to which he later turned.

---

[25]Richard Ripple, Robert E. Biehler, and Gail A. Jaquish, <u>Human Development</u>, 44-45, 50-51, 63-64; Erik Erikson, <u>The Life Cycle Completed: A Review</u> (New York: W. W. Norton & Co., 1982), 32-33; Leonie Sugarman, <u>Life-Span Development: Concepts, Theories and Interventions</u>, 85; Louis Breger, <u>From Instinct to Identity: The Development of Personality</u>, 9, 289; Paul B. Baltes and K. Warner Schaie, eds., <u>Life-Span Developmental Psychology: Personality and Socialization</u> (New York: Academic Press, 1973), 9; Lawrence Kohlberg, <u>Essays on Moral Development</u>, vol. 1, <u>The Philosophy of Moral Development: Moral Stages and the Idea of Justice</u> (San Francisco: Harper & Row, Publishers, 1981), 128; James Fowler, <u>Stages of Faith: The Psychology of Human Development and the Quest for Meaning</u>, 52, 113.

LIFE-STAGE AGES		FREUD'S PSYCHO-SEXUAL STAGES	PIAGET'S COGNITIVE STAGES	ERIKSON'S PSYCHO-SOCIAL STAGES	KOHLBERG'S MORAL STAGES	FOWLER'S FAITH STAGES
Infancy Birth thru 1 Year		1 Oral Stage Feeding	1 Sensorimotor Physical Sense	1-Basic Trust vs. Basic Mistrust HOPE		Undifferen-tiated Faith
Early Child-hood 2 thru 3 Years		2 Anal Stage Toilet Training	2 Intuitive/ Preopera-tional Thinking, Basic Symbolism	2-Autonomy vs. Shame, Doubt WILL		1 Intuitive-Projective Faith
Play Age 4 thru 5 Years		3 Phallic Stage Sexual Difference		3-Initiative vs. Guilt PURPOSE	*PreConven-tional* - 1 Obedience, Punishment	
School Age 6 thru 11 Years		Latency Period	3 Concrete, Differen-tiated Literal Thought	4-Industry vs. Inferiority COMPETENCE	*PreConven-tional* - 2 Naively Egoistic	2 Mythic-Literal Faith
Adoles-cence 12 to 18 Years		4 Genital Stage Completion	4 Formal, Abstract Thought	5-Identity vs. Identity Confusion FIDELITY	*Conventional* 3 *Approval*	3 Synthetic-Conventional Faith
Young Adult-hood 18 to 35 Years				6-Intimacy vs. Isolation LOVE	*Conventional* 4 - Law & Order / *Post-Conven-tional* 5 Contractual Legalistic	4 Individuative-Reflective Faith
Adult-hood 35 to 65 Years				7-Generativity vs. Stagnation CARE	*Post-Conventional* 6	5 Conjunctive Faith
Old Age 65+ Years				8-Integrity vs. Despair WISDOM	Conscience or Principled	6 Universalizing Faith

Figure 1: Areas of Developmental Life Stages

In the area of psychology Freud developed the new field of scientific inquiry, psychoanalysis, which is a controlled method of delving into the internal aspect of individuals, the unconscious mind, which he believed has a powerful influence on conscious thought. He set aside hypnosis and used the controlled method of "free association" using patients' cooperation in introspection along with empathy to bring out, from the unconscious mind to the conscious, reasons for the patients' actions.

Technically, Freud believed there were three levels of consciousness in individuals, the conscious, entailing mental processes a person is aware of at a particular moment; the preconscious, pertaining to memories which can be readily recalled; and the unconscious, involving memories which cannot be recalled except in unusual circumstances such as in dreams, hypnosis or free associations. Conflicts among these levels of consciousness caused many types of behavior according to Freud. He believed these conflicts stemmed from the makeup of one's personality containing the *id, ego,* and *superego*. The *id* was considered to be completely unconscious and the source of one's basic instinctual drive or energy; the *ego* was considered to be partially conscious and partially unconscious, controlling the energy of the *id*; and the *superego* was considered to be one's conscience.[26]

Freud approached his psychoanalysis psychology from a biological perspective, believing in the idea that sexuality developed through sequential stages from infancy to adulthood and that this sexuality was a driving force in persons' actions.[27] In fact, he saw sexuality as the key with which to understand human nature, emphasizing it over other important factors.[28] His idea of sexuality included pleasurable types of sensations, not just what would pertain to the sex.

---

[26]Leonie Sugarman, Life-Span Development: Concepts, Theories and Interventions, 46-47.

[27]Academic American Encyclopedia, 1993 ed., s.v. "Freud, Sigmund"; Louis Breger, From Instinct to Identity: The Development of Personality (Englewood Cliffs, NJ: Prentice-Hall, Inc., 1974), 6.

[28]David O. Yates, What the Bible Says About Your Personality, 1.

Freud labeled his idea of sexuality as the *libido*, considering it the basic instinctual energy in each individual which comes from the *id*. One's *libido* energy would often concentrate on a particular part of the body involving primary drives such as hunger, thirst, cleanliness, or sex. The *libido* was considered to focus on various parts of the body at different age levels. This idea became classified by Freud into psychosexual developmental stages.[29] Note Figure 1 for a comparison of Erikson's life stage ages with Freud's psychosexual stages.

Freud's psychosexual developmental stages parallel Erikson's with respect to age divisions up to young adulthood with their development being considered complete sometime during adolescence. Problems which occur in the adulthood through old-age stages usually are attributed to problems in psychosexual development prior to its completion in development. As the chart indicates, the stages pertain to libidinal focus on body areas which is quite limiting with respect to behavior causes.

In essence, Freud's approach attempts to explain causes for aberrant behavior but offered no positive help for healing. And his approach is too rigid and categorical, attempting to explain behavior from but a few questionable influences, but this is understandable considering his background of biological medical science which usually has reliable, predictable patterns. Many of Freud's associates pulled away from him because of his narrow emphasis on sexuality. Freud's psychosexual ideas may explain some behavior, especially in the physical and biological realm of growth, but they fail to explain other types of developmental behavior adequately because they acknowledge influences basically in the limited area of sexuality.

---

[29]Richard Ripple, Robert F. Biehler, and Gail A. Jaquish, <u>Human Development</u>, 44; Louis Breger, <u>From Instinct to Identity: The Development of Personality</u>, 16; Paul B. Baltes and K. Warner Schaie, eds., <u>Life-Span Developmental Psychology: Personality and Socialization</u>, 18.

<u>Piaget - Cognitive</u>

Jean Piaget was born in Neuchatel, Switzerland, on August 9, 1896 and died on September 17, 1980. He had an interest in biology as did Freud and became engaged in biological research at an early age. After receiving his Ph.D. in this area, he combined this interest with studies in epistemology, for which he became noted, especially with respect to how children learn and develop cognitively. He approached these studies from the view that intelligence is grounded in the concept of biological adaptation. Consequently, it became natural for him to recognize and set forth stages of intellectual development from birth through adulthood. In fact, he proposed that development occurs in genetically determined stages which always follow the same sequence.[30] This dogmatic approach does not leave much room for variation and individuality but provides a framework for comparison, nonetheless. His stages are included in Figure 1.

Piaget observed that in the first stage the infants and young children accumulate understanding of themselves and the world around them through their senses and motor activities. This early understanding helps them engage in mental and physical trial and error behavior. In the next stage, children's thinking involves symbols such as words which enable them to gain from what they have already learned. Here concentration is on only one quality at a time without the ability to mentally reverse actions. Thinking in the third stage is not as limiting as earlier. However, though the child now is capable of mentally reversing actions, thinking is limited to what the child can actually see or has actually experienced concretely and directly. In the final stage, children are able to generalize and think in abstract and hypothetical terms as well as introspect and deal with a shift in time perspectives. This stage is referred to as formal since it involves structured or form thinking. Early in this stage, generalized thinking is

---

[30]<u>Academic American Encyclopedia</u>, s.v. "Piaget, Jean"; <u>Concise Columbia Encyclopedia</u>, 1989 ed., s.v. "Piaget, Jean."

more or less haphazard, but it gradually develops into a systematic, organized process.[31]

The main features of Piaget's developmental model of cognitive stages are as follows: the order of the stages of development is invariable, each stage is vital and cannot be skipped, each stage is more complex and a transformation of the previous stage, each stage is foundational to and preparation for the next stage.[32] Although these stages have received much criticism due to their invariant, ordered structure, "hundreds of psychologists have carried out impeccably scientific studies to test many of Piaget's hypotheses and have supplied impressive evidence to lend support to many of his basic arguments."[33] Even though his stages are ordered and deemed necessary in the cognitive process, Piaget does acknowledge variation occurs in the beginning and length of the stages with respect to the correlation of children's ages, but the relationship of his stages to ages appears to be the most common grouping according to observation.

In addition to his cognitive stages, Piaget also proposed a theory for the nature of operational thought. He saw it as a procedure which involved organization, adaptation, assimilation, accommodation, and equilibration. In the process of thinking, according to this theory, one first attempts to organize outside input or experience into an understandable system (or organization), then the input is transformed (or adapted) into a usable manner or form from the individual's perspective in order to deal with new experiences (assimilation). When input or experience cannot be adapted into a usable manner by an individual based upon the current perception, the individual may have to transform or conform to the new experience or reality as it is then perceived (accommodation). The stabilizing process (equilibrium) of either

---

[31]Richard Ripple, Robert F. Biehler, and Gail A. Jaquish, Human Development, 61-64; Louis Breger, From Instinct to Identity: The Development of Personality, 267.

[32]Louis Breger, From Instinct to Identity: The Development of Personality, 9.

[33]Richard Ripple, Robert F. Biehler, and Gail A. Jaquish, Human Development, 61-64, 65.

assimilation or accommodation is considered natural to this type of ordered thinking which attempts to bring understanding and balance to one's perception of the world and to inconsistent experiences.[34]

This whole nature of operational thought is considered to cause growth and development as one interacts with the world. It also is referred to as "egocentrism" which expands perspectives and causes growth from one stage of cognitive development to the next. It is not necessarily a concept which pertains to selfishness or self-centeredness but carries the idea of self-viewing the world intellectually and making understanding of it in a meaningful way back to the self. As this process occurs, imbalance and then equilibrium transpire with growth to the next stage resulting from extended ranges of experience. In experiences, the tendency is to view the world solely from one's own perspective and understanding. But when inconsistencies of perspectives occur and then when one allows stretching of understanding and consideration of others' viewpoints and desires to bring back the equilibrium, growth takes place, stage development occurs, and there is tempering of egocentrism.[35] The idea can be diagrammed as follows:

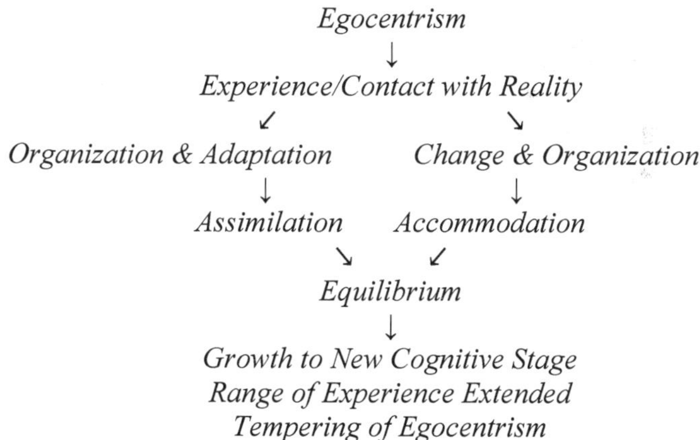

Figure 2: Tempering of Egocentrism

---

[34]Ibid., 56-59.

[35]Louis Breger, <u>From Instinct to Identity: The Development of Personality</u>, 9-10.

Piaget's theories are helpful in understanding how children think and learn and behave, however, they only present a few perspectives. Many other influences have a part in this developmental process. Nonetheless, they do help to guide our understanding and have provided foundational bases from which many other theorists have begun their work. It is a fact that Freud and Piaget are mentioned much more often (way over double) in recent psychology journals than any other psychologist.[36] This indicates the tremendous contribution they have made in their field.

Erikson - Psychosocial

Erik Erikson was born in Germany on June 15, 1902, studied in Vienna at Freud's Vienna Psychoanalytic Institute, and emigrated to the United States in 1933. He came to be one of the leading psychoanalysts and theorists on human development and was among the first to study the behavior and function of healthy people.[37]

As would be imagined, Freud had a great impact on Erikson, with respect to psychoanalysis and life stages. However, Erikson did not allow Freud's ideas to limit him but continued on to study the process of growing up in many cultures and social settings. He expanded the idea of life stages to take in the whole life span involving eight stages rather than Freud's five and reshaped Freud's psychosexual stages into psychosocial stages, which still utilize the physical developmental model but include psychological, social, and interpersonal considerations. Erikson's eight life stages of development are "the most widely known and widely quoted account of the life cycle in the social science literature." They are actually a model "of a changing individual operating in a

---

[36]Richard Ripple, Robert F. Biehler, and Gail A. Jaquish, <u>Human Development</u>, 64.

[37]<u>Academic American Encyclopedia</u>, s.v. "Erikson, Erik."

changing society," the result of change and development being influenced by both the individual and culture.[38]

Erikson's life-stage ages are the basis for comparison used in this paper. Figure 1 shows the actual psychosocial stages of Erikson alongside the other stages.

Erikson contends that the development of an individual is a cumulative process based upon a timetable of relative ages. He has divided his timetable into eight stages which involve psychosocial tasks or crises as noted in the chart above. The stages indicate crises which are listed as polar opposites but actually represent dimensions and degrees rather than options. The outcome of a stage can range between the polar opposites. The cause of growth to each successive stage is seen to occur as the result of societal demands to which a person must adapt but which cause an emotional crisis which needs resolving. As the crisis is resolved, it leads into the entrance of the next stage and takes with it the dimension of the polar opposite crisis which was the result of the crisis resolution from the last stage experienced. Although each stage has its own period of prominence and is based upon the sequential stages before it, Erikson acknowledges that each stage exists in a fashion throughout life and may be dealt with at any time. Therefore, a person may continue to address the crisis type involved in a developmental area or task stage whether or not it is in the life stage of prominence. Consequently, detrimental development is not irreversible; there is hope for improvement. However, regression also is possible. Thus, the developmental process becomes complex and interrelated.[39]

Adding to the complexity of stage development is Erikson's concept of epigenetic development which ties together the biological processes of the body in organismic growth with social development as having an interrelated part

---

[38]Leonie Sugarman, <u>Life-Span Development: Concepts, Theories and Interventions</u>, 83-84; Louis Breger, <u>From Instinct to Identity: The Development of Personality</u>, 8.

[39]Leonie Sugarman, <u>Life-Span Development: Concepts, Theories and Interventions</u>, 84.

in human behavior and individuality or personality. Epigenesis technically is a biological term which indicates that in the embryo "each organ has its time of origin" and prominence or ascendancy when it develops, and each should develop at its proper time and contribute by its proper size and function to the effective working of the whole system. Erikson believes that the same principle of epigenesis at work in the embryo should continue to work after birth, contributing toward the healthy growth of the individual at a proper "normal" or "average-expectable" rate and sequence for the healthy development of "physical, cognitive, and social capabilities." As Erikson notes, epigenesis

> by no means signifies a mere succession. It also determines certain laws in the fundamental relations of the growing parts to each other. . . . Each part exists in some form before "its" decisive and critical time normally arrives and remains systematically related to all others so that the whole ensemble depends on the proper development in the proper sequence of each item. Finally, as each part comes to its full ascendance and finds some lasting solution during its stage [of prominence] it will also be expected to develop further under the dominance of subsequent ascendancies and most of all, to take its place in the integration of the whole ensemble.[40]

The epigenetic-type growth after birth and during the life stages, then as noted above, does allow for development of a stage outside of its vital season of dominance or ascendancy since each stage is considered to exist in some fashion at the beginning and throughout the life span.

Along with Erikson's crises or tasks in stage development, he also identifies a word at each stage which represents the psychosocial strength or desired ego or personality quality which should be produced as the healthy process of development occurs. These positive qualities or virtues should

---

[40]Erik Erikson, <u>The Life Cycle Completed: A Review</u>, 26-29.

emerge from the successful results of the respective crisis conflicts of each stage but depend upon the dimension of the resolution of the crisis conflicts themselves.

James Fowler has created a fictional conversation between the theorists Lawrence Kohlberg, Jean Piaget, and Erik Erikson. The following is an excerpt from his fictional statement by Erik Erikson which sums up the ideas of Erikson mentioned above.

Epigenesis combines an understanding of development as the unfolding or emergence, on schedule, of new organ modes or capacities with an additional dimension. . . . Epigenesis as a concept also refers the innovative or adaptive responses a post-natal organism makes to the challenges and opportunities its environment provides. Epigenetic stages, then, describe the emergence of new capacities and the leeway they provide for individuating organismal adaptation, and point to the limits or distortions to which the failure to appear on schedule give rise. . . . Therefore, when I speak of a psychosocial stage, I refer to a phase of development marked by significant bodily changes, accompanied by emotional and cognitive growth, giving rise to new relational modes and roles in the context of institutional arrangements geared to meet, form and utilize the person's new capacities and accompanying new 'sense of self.' . . . Each new stage is initiated by a crisis; a struggle between the optimal possibilities presented by one's emerging new capacities, on the one hand, and the failure to integrate them into one's being and well-being on the other. The stages are cumulative in that one brings to each new crisis the mixed residue of past solutions. Each new stage requires the reworking of those past solutions and contains in it an anticipation of the issues of crises in future stages.[41]

In viewing this imaginary statement, it is evident that there is the idea of hope throughout the stages, hope for improvement in a stage area even when the ascendancy of a particular stage is past because the stages are interrelated though sequential. Hope is the virtuous quality which arises, according to Erikson, through the successful resolution of the crisis of the first stage. The first stage is in Infancy and deals with the crisis of Basic Trust versus Basic Mistrust. During this period, if development is healthy, one gains a basic sense of trust and confidence in self through the consistency of normal bodily functions working properly such as breathing, eating, digesting, and eliminating. At the same time, one can gain a feeling of predictability from the environment such as being cared for adequately with respect to the needs of nourishment, warmth, cleanliness, and comfort. With a healthy body and healthy environment, a positive degree of trust develops which is carried into the sequential stages of development providing Hope and anticipation for positive results in the future. If experience in the first stage is not positive, a degree of mistrust develops along with a lessened degree of hope for positive future eventualities. In this first stage, the beginning sense of one's ego or personality identity develops. As Erikson indicates, the personality is seen in the statement, "I am what I am given."[42] Resolution of the first-stage crisis pertaining to trust of self and environment, no matter the degree, leads to the second stage.

The second psychosocial stage, which is in Early Childhood, involves Autonomy versus Shame and Doubt, the resolution of which leads to Will. Because the child has developed physically to the extent he or she can move about

---

[41] James W. Fowler, <u>Stages of Faith: The Psychology of Human Develop-ment and the Quest for Meaning</u> (San Francisco: Harper & Row, Publishers, 1981), 48.

[42] Leonie Sugarman, <u>Life-Span Development: Concepts, Theories and Interventions</u>, 86, 88.

more freely than when an infant, the child experiences a sense of limited freedom and independence. During this stage, a child needs an adequate amount of freedom and control, allowing opportunity for some choices which can foster development of self-control and self-esteem. Too much control or too little causes hindrance to self-esteem and stifles the child's ability to exercise his Will properly. This leads to shame and doubt and feelings of inadequacy. The child at this stage needs to begin to develop and realize his or her identity by learning how to use his or her Will along acceptable guidelines and parameters. Personality centers around, "I am what I will."[43] Resolution of this crisis of handling freedom and control leads to the third stage.

The third stage is the Play Age which deals with Initiative versus Guilt and leads to Purpose. In this stage, children have a greater sense of themselves as persons than in the previous stages. This leads to the playful acting out of prospective future roles in imitative play, often copying the roles of their parents. This play acting shows initiative, a free sense of enterprise according to Erikson. Conscience is considered to be a dominant part of initiative which encourages individual dependability. However, along with the development of conscience comes the potential for guilt. Guilt can be a good quality, an encouragement for morality; however, its feeling can be overburdensome as a result of the heavy condemnation of others. When excessive condemnation occurs, initiative is often stifled. But when conscience is healthy, initiative is free to show itself and a sense of identity and Purpose begins to surface. A person's personality and individuality become evident in initiative, a person thinking on his or her own, which develops Purpose. The personality revolves around, "I am what I can imagine I will be."[44]

The fourth stage is the School Age of Industry versus Inferiority from which Competence comes. Here, the individual faces the need to learn the specific physical and intellectual tools or technology of society in order to function effectively

---

[43]Ibid., 86-87, 88.

[44]Ibid., 87-88.

therein. With healthy adjustment in this learning process, the individual develops a sense of industry through proper use of the tools. However, if there are problems in this learning process or if there are problems of adjustment and inadequacy from insufficient resolutions in the previous stages, feelings of inferiority will result. In this stage, then, a sense of adequate or inadequate Competence regarding one's ability to function in society results from the crisis of learning society's tools. The personality is seen as, "I am what I learn," at this stage.[45]

Adolescence is the fifth stage for which Erikson is famous. In this stage, the crisis of Identity and Identity Confusion lead to Fidelity. At this period, the individual experiences rapid physical and hormonal changes which can cause confusion with respect to the physical sameness and consistency that has been experienced earlier. Security with what is familiar is lost and the need for a new sameness and consistency presents itself. Of critical importance are sexual and occupational identities. The individual wants to know, "Who am I?" "How do I fit into the world?" "What is my future?" At this stage, the virtues of the previous stages are reconsidered and reworked into the new perspective of what the individual is becoming and what is becoming meaningful to the individual as he or she considers taking a meaningful place in the world. This leads to Fidelity or faithfulness to what is becoming meaningful. Thus, stability of identity becomes important. As a result, often an individual will identify with a cause, either good or bad, in order to establish a definite identity. Fidelity to the cause or identity often becomes strong. However, if instability remains at this stage, identity and role confusion result and one has little in which to place Fidelity.[46] But with a sense and security of identity, one becomes faithful to the cause of identity. Here the personality appears to be, I am that with which I identify.

Young Adulthood is stage six, in which the crisis of Intimacy versus Isolation (distantiation and self-absorption)

---

[45]Ibid., 88.

[46]Ibid., 88-89.

leads to Love. This stage calls for self-abandonment and giving of oneself in intimacy to another. In order to do this successfully, one must have a clear and established identity of self from the previous stage and release the self-absorption accompanying the establishment of identity identification by merging identity intimately with another. The risk is that individual identity will be lost, but the benefit is that it will be enhanced in the giving through intimacy. The crisis of releasing focus on self and entering into self-givingness through intimacy leads to Love. Those who cannot enter into an intimate, self-abandoned relationship often isolate themselves from closeness with others.[47] It becomes hard for them to give and receive love though they may desire it. Erikson notes that commitment is necessary in the association of intimacy of love, and sacrifices and compromises are required.[48] This may be difficult for some also. Actual Love should not stifle the one loved but should enjoy the other's uniqueness and should seek to bring out the best in the other. At this stage, the personality that is secure and is able to give of self can be considered as the following, What I am I merge with another (or others).

The seventh stage is Adulthood which involves the crisis of Generativity versus Stagnation and leads to Care. At this stage in life, the healthy individual evaluates his or her life and desires that it have meaning, the insights of which can be taught and passed along to the next generation. Generativity, then, has to do with the idea of providing generating insight into learned truths and what is deemed to be important by establishing or teaching or producing the insights in those who are younger. By so doing, one's life has not been a waste; it takes on meaning and significance because what has been learned can be passed on to the next generation. This stage shows the importance of the interdependence of the generations. Those who reach this stage of life and do not look outward but inward, often reach stagnation and are pre-occupied with self. At this point, life seems futile. The virtue

---

[47]Ibid., 89-90.

[48]Erik Erikson, <u>The Life Cycle Completed: A Review</u>, 70.

resulting from the crisis at this stage is Care, care for the welfare of others and sharing what one has learned that is meaningful for their benefit. This is the result of a healthy generativity which Erikson states, "always invites the possibility of an energetic shift to *productivity* and *creativity* in the service of the generations."[49] A perspective of personality at this stage can be, What I am I share.

The eighth and last stage is Old Age which deals with the crisis of Integrity versus Despair and leads to the quality of Wisdom. Integrity pertains to the integrity of oneself with respect to acceptance of self and of the dignity of the life one has led with the knowledge that it is one's own responsibility. It portrays contentment with one's own life as one faces the soon reality of experiencing death. Contentment at this stage is the result of successful resolutions of the previous seven crisis periods. The contented person is happy with self and identity and has lived a meaningful life, contributing to significant input in the lives of those who make up the next generation. If a person at this stage is not happy with self or the life lived, Despair and often disgust are evident because his or her life is now too short to become meaningful and make a difference for the benefit of others. However, Wisdom results in the person who has successfully resolved this crisis period and those periods which were before.[50] The dictionary definitions of Wisdom are as follows: "understanding of what is true, right, or lasting; common sense; good judgment";[51] "the power of true and right discernment; also, conformity to the course of action dictated by such discernment."[52] Therefore, Wisdom, as the result of this stage crisis, involves discernment of life along with living according to the discernment while providing understanding of what is deemed to

---

[49]Leonie Sugarman, Life-Span Development: Concepts, Theories and Interventions, 90-92; Erik Erikson, The Life Cycle Completed: A Review, 53.

[50]Leonie Sugarman, Life-Span Development: Concepts, Theories and Interventions, 92-94.

[51]American Heritage Dictionary, s.v. "Wisdom."

[52]The Reader's Digest Great Encyclopedic Encyclopedia, s.v. "Wisdom."

be meaningful so it will last as it is given to others. Integrity of self leads to Wisdom. Erikson comments about integrity, seeing it as "a sense of *coherence* and *wholeness*," an "integrality" or "integrative experience of earlier stages [which has] come to fruition" which allows "for the gradual maturation of integrity."[53] Consequently in this final stage, an appropriate personality description for the healthy person's life experience is, What I am has meaning.

As is evident, Erikson's psychosocial stages are concerned with the personality which is seen to develop throughout life. A concept of one's identity reflected through personality is healthy as one is content with self and interacts with society and contributes in a meaningful way.

Kohlberg - Moral

Lawrence Kohlberg launched research in moral development over thirty years ago, beginning in the 1950's. His research was more concerned about the process of moral reasoning, how people think and what reasons they give for their moral determinations, rather than what they think. As a result of his studies, he identified six universal stages which occur in the process of moral development. As Piaget and Erikson, Kohlberg's stages are sequential and in invariant order; each previous stage is deemed foundational for the next stage. And each succeeding stage is more complex and differentiated, becoming a transformation of the previous stages.[54]

Figure 1 charts Kohlberg's six stages of moral development alongside the other developmental stages. Kohlberg actually acknowledges three levels of moral development with each level having two stages. The first level is the *Pre-Conventional* level in which a child considers moral actions as good or bad based upon the physical consequences of

---

[53]Erik Erikson, <u>The Life Cycle Completed: A Review</u>, 65.

[54]Leonie Sugarman, <u>Life-Span Development: Concepts, Theories and Interventions</u>, 70; Louis Breger, <u>From Instinct to Identity: The Development of Personality</u>, 275-279; Paul B. Baltes and K. Warner Schaie, eds., <u>Life-Span Developmental Psychology: Personality and Socialization</u>, 179.

reward and punishment. In the first stage of this level, Obedience and Punishment, a child attempts to act so as to avoid punishment or so as not to get caught in what are considered wrong actions. In the second stage, Naively Egoistic, the child still tries to avoid punishment but also attempts to act in order to receive rewards or reciprocal benefits.[55]

The second level is the *Conventional* level in which moral actions are considered good or bad according to the degree they conform to the expectations of one's family, group, or nation. Conformity, loyalty and identification with the esteemed group are important moral actions at this stage, regardless of the consequence of actions. The first stage of this level, then, is Approval. Here one wants to please and help others, seeking their approval. Also, the idea of intention enters into the consideration of the degree of goodness of moral actions. Law and Order is the second stage of this level. In this stage, right behavior involves respecting authority and maintaining the social order. This is to be done for its own sake; again, the idea of intention is considered.[56]

Post-Conventional is the third level in which one's own standards of moral behavior are developed irrespective of the views of others and of authority. Here, the first stage is Contractual Legalistic wherein one's conscience is active with respect to what is fair in society. Therefore, individual rights are considered but personal values and opinions are deemed relative as they fit into what is best for the majority in society as a whole. In this regard, effort is made to reach a mutual consensus or free agreement or contract to which one is considered obligated. The second stage involves the Conscience with respect to the Universal Ethical Principle. Personal responsibility is assumed for actions in accordance with self-chosen, universally ethical principles, principles which are the abstract type of the Golden Rule, which consider

---

[55]Lawrence Kohlberg, The Philosophy of Moral Development: Moral Stages and the Idea of Justice, 17.

[56]Ibid., 18.

justice and the equality of human rights as well as individual human dignity.[57]

In order to help understand Kohlberg's six stages of moral development, he provided the following descriptions of the stages with respect to a moral aspect. The first aspect pertains to obedience of rules:

1. Obey rules to avoid punishment.
2. Conform to obtain rewards, have favors returned, and so on.
3. Conform to avoid disapproval and dislike by others.
4. Conform to avoid censure by legitimate authorities and resultant guilt.
5. Conform to maintain the respect of the impartial spectator judging in terms of community welfare.
6. Conform to avoid self-condemnation.

The second aspect deals with the value of human life:

1. The value of human life is confused with the value of physical objects and is based on the social status or physical attributes of the possessor.
2. The value of human life is seen as instrumental to the satisfaction of the needs of its possessor or of other people.
3. The value of human life is based on the empathy and affection of family members and others toward its possessor.
4. Life is conceived as sacred in terms of its place in a categorical moral or religious order of rights and duties.
5. Life is valued both in terms of its relation to community welfare and in terms of life being a universal human right.
6. Human life is sacred—a universal human value of respect for the individual.[58]

---

[57] Ibid., 18-19.
[58] Ibid., 19-20.

As one grows in the process of moral development, the growth becomes dependent upon and related to cognitive growth as well because logical understanding of self and the rights of others is involved in moral reasoning and behavior as noted in Kohlberg's descriptions above. Kohlberg also notes that, as moral development progresses, a gradual de-centering occurs as one begins to see the viewpoints and perspectives of others.[59] As a result, virtue develops which Kohlberg defines as justice and the "knowledge of the good."[60] However, he also makes the statement, "He who knows the good chooses the good."[61] It does appear that virtue develops through the process of moral development and that cognitive development is a necessary and complementary factor, but because a person has acquired personal values of morality and a personal concept of correct behavior which may be considered in the area of universally ethical principles, this in no way guarantees corresponding behavior by that person. Many other factors influence behavior besides the influence of one's knowledge even though it is based on universally ethical principles which one believes are valid and good. Actions often are committed in a fit of anger even when one knows that the actions will violate his or her moral values. But emotion is not always at fault; a reversion to self-centered-ness or egocentrism may cause one to become unethical with full knowledge of the inequity of the action. Arriving at Kohlberg's sixth moral stage of development with the accompanying acquisition of a developed virtue of justice and goodness does not verify that a person will always act accordingly. If it did, there would be some people in the world who would be just about perfect, and they have not been discovered (yet).

---

[59] Louis Breger, From Instinct to Identity: The Development of Person-ality, 277-278.

[60] The American Heritage Dictionary, s.v. "Virtue," defines Virtue as "Moral excellence and righteousness; goodness."

[61] Lawrence Kohlberg, The Philosophy of Moral Development: Moral Stages and the Idea of Justice, *xxix*; Louis Breger, From Instinct to Identity: The Development of Personality, 279.

Fowler- Faith

Lawrence Kohlberg comments that James Fowler's "pioneering work on faith development, based on a wealth of empirical research, has opened up a whole new area in the study of human development . . . [and indicates] how the meaning of one's life can change and develop over a lifetime."[62] Much of Fowler's work fits the same pattern of Kohlberg's moral development stages as well as those of Piaget's cognitive and Erikson's psychosocial stages.[63] Fowler's stages of faith are considered to be sequential stages as are theirs, and as Erikson and Kohlberg, Fowler believes his faith stages cover the whole life span. Also, he comments that not all people reach the maturity of the last stage, which is sixth, but reach a plateau in other stages. In studying the progression of faith, Fowler is more concerned about the process of faith rather than content or object of faith. He notes that all people have a type of faith since, to him, faith provides the reason for living, the meaning and sense of life. "More verb than noun, faith is the dynamic system of images, values, and commitments that guides one's life. It is thus universal: everyone who chooses to go on living operates by some basic faith."[64] Fowler's faith stages appear on Figure 1.

When one faces the reality and finality of death, faith becomes necessary and meaningful. Facing the idea of death makes one think about one's life and its significance. It, there-fore, encourages one to find meaning and purpose to life. It was Fowler's experience as he contemplated death. It brought him face to face with faith according to his perspective which he states, "is our way of finding coherence in and giving meaning to the multiple forces and relations that make up our lives." Therefore, it influences our behavior. "It shapes the

---

[62]James Fowler, <u>Stages of Faith: The Psychology of Human Develop-</u><u>ment and the Quest for Meaning</u>, back of jacket cover.

[63]In fact, Fowler gives Erikson credit for the foundation upon which he builds, "Erikson's work has become part of the interpretative mind-set I bring to research on faith development." James Fowler, <u>Stages of Faith: The Psychology of Human Development and the Quest for Meaning</u>, 110.

[64]Ibid., inside front jacket cover.

ways we invest our deepest loves and our most costly loyalties."[65] "It involves an alignment of the will, a resting of the heart, in accordance with a vision of transcendent value and power, one's ultimate concern."[66] The object of the vision is considered to have "intrinsic excellence and worth," and helps to shape one's identity as it is the focal point of one's faith and commitment.[67] Faith is not necessarily religious, although it may be.

Faith attempts to give coherence to life's experiences and to provide them with meaning. Fowler believes it is natural to seek meaning, therefore, natural to have faith, and proposes that the capacity for faith is present at birth.[68] Agreeing with Erikson's first psychosocial stage of Basic Trust versus Basic Mistrust, Fowler comments that faith takes "form in our earliest relationships with those who provide care for us in infancy."[69] He calls this the pre-stage of Undifferentiated faith. In it seeds are sown which will affect later faith development, seeds of faith as one begins to trust and relate to others. When thought and language begin to formulate, transition to the first actual stage of faith development begins which corresponds to Piaget's second stage.[70]

Thought and language help the child to use symbols for meaning in communication and play acting. This leads to the first stage of Intuitive-Projective faith. In this stage, the beginning of arranging experience into meaningful units occurs, although thought patterns change often. Usually the child makes use of the imagination and fantasies, unhindered by logical thought processes. The child becomes aware of self at this stage and is egocentric, not able to perceive the perspectives of others. Transition to the next stage occurs when

---

[65]Ibid., *xi*, 4, 5.

[66]Ibid., 14.

[67]Ibid., 18.

[68]Ibid., *xiii.*

[69]Ibid., 5.

[70]Ibid., 121.

the child attains the ability to think concretely according to Piaget's cognitive developmental third stage.[71]

In the second stage of Mythic-Literal faith, though the child still uses stories to communicate understanding of experiences and meanings, he or she attempts to sort the real from the unreal. The stories usually reflect the symbolic but literal beliefs of the person's community. During this stage, the world seems to take on a predictable order, and at the same time, perspectives of others also are considered. At this stage one thinks linearly and concretely, using literal interpretation with respect to moral rules and beliefs and considering the fairness of reciprocal justice. As one develops the ability to use formal operational thought indicated in Piaget's fourth stage, transition to the next stage transpires.[72]

The next stage is the third stage, Synthetic-Conventional faith, in which one begins to notice the inconsistencies of literal, concrete thinking and now is able to reflect upon meanings through the use of formal operational thought.[73] There is a desire to know God (or the "unifying power of the ultimate environment," if not God) in a personal way and to see God as transcendent yet immanent (far superior yet involved in human lives), who knows the individual and others in the depths of their beings. Individual identity becomes important in this stage as many changes are taking place in development and one tries to formulate a concept of his or her own personality. It, therefore, is encouraging to view God as the One who knows the individual better than one knows oneself. Also, other spheres become dominant besides family, such as school, friends, community, and religion. Now the individual attempts to develop a unifying perspective which faith can provide as it "synthesizes values and information," giving a basis for identity. However, one's values often are related to and in conformity with what is expected by others, but they lack the development of an independent perspective from personal reflection. Here, one has the ability to conceive

---

[71]Ibid., 133-134.

[72]Ibid., 135-136, 149.

[73]Ibid., 150.

abstractly and to imagine ideals. This can result in overly idealistic concepts, which consider a group or institution as perfect, or overly judgmental attitudes based upon a conceived ideal. This is the stage in which many become comfortable and remain throughout the rest of their lives. When stage transition does occur, it results from critical reflection upon the previously held beliefs with a reevaluation of how they came to be and of their relativity in light of the individual's group and background.[74]

In stage four, Individuative-Reflective faith, the focus of authority changes from external sources to the self. Although other authorities are considered, the individual becomes the final authority for personal choices and decisions which determine lifestyle, beliefs and attitudes and accepts the responsibility accompanying them. Fowler calls this decision-making power of the individual's authority the *executive ego*. As meanings are reflected upon at this stage, a *demythologizing* takes place in which meanings are separated from the symbols which represent them. This can enhance the meanings of symbols to a greater extent since the reasons behind the symbols can be expressed in deeper clarity through the vehicle of words besides the limited symbols. Here, symbols are not used or revered for their own sakes but are seen as vehicles and can take on greater depth of meaning as the meaning is distinguished from them and becomes explicit. As a result of the critical thinking of reflective demythologizing, one develops a self-certainty and a self-identity as well as a world-outlook identity. If there is transition to the next stage, it occurs when one becomes dissatisfied with one's established self-identity and world outlook and realizes life is not as neat and orderly as defined in stage four but is more elaborate, complex and multilevel.[75]

Stage five is complex even to define. Fowler calls it Conjunctive faith and describes it with several analogies. Two of them follow:

---

[74]Ibid., 151-154, 172-173.

[75]Ibid., 179-183.

> Discovering that the rational solution or "ex-
> planation" of a problem that seemed so elegant
> is but a painted canvas covering an intricate,
> endlessly intriguing cavern of surprising depth.

> Looking at a field of flowers simultaneously
> through a microscope and a wide-angle lens.[76]

This is not an "either/or" stage of reasoning but attempts to see the pattern of interrelatedness in the many sides of an issue or concept. It involves what Fowler terms *dialogical* knowing which allows and welcomes dialogue from the "multiplex structure of the world." This stage realizes "that truth is more multidimensional and organically interdependent than most theories or accounts of truth can grasp." Therefore, the symbols which have been demythologized in stage four are now seen as inadequate to convey deeper aspects of truth. Consequently, the person at stage five is open to dialogue from other perspectives, with the possibility of gaining new insights to truth without sacrificing one's own commitment to one's perceived truth. In fact, other claims to truth are evaluated and tested in light of one's own experience of truth. "Conjunctive faith's radical openness to the truth of the other stems precisely from its confidence in the reality mediated by its own tradition and in the awareness that that reality over-spills its mediation." Valuable insights may be gained from others of differing opinions regarding truth whether or not one accepts all of another's perspective. Also, a *second naïvete* occurs as symbols now are seen in unity with their conceptual meanings, giving depth to the reality they represent; this is the interrelatedness typical of this stage. One's past also is considered, here, with the attempt to critically recognize areas of value and to integrate them into one's perspective. Thus, one's past is seen to be important in the process of development. As past and present are incorporated into multilevel, interrelated perspectives of self and the world, Erikson's seventh stage of Generativity comes

---

[76]Ibid., 184.

into view. One now wants to share meaningful truths which have been gleaned from life to help others on their journey. As Fowler states, "this stage is ready to spend and be spent for the cause of conserving and cultivating the possibility of others' generating identity and meaning." It is not often that individuals progress to this stage, and it is even less often that one advances to Fowler's stage six of "radical actualization." However, stage five has some inconsistencies with respect to what one believes to be truth and how one interacts with society. Here, one adapts one's truth or compromises it in order to work within society as it is, seeking to maintain the status quo with respect to self and well-being.[77] In the next stage, one attempts to transform society.

Stage six is Fowler's last stage of faith development which he calls Universalizing faith. This stage coincides with Erikson's eighth stage, his last also, called Integrity versus Despair which should lead to Wisdom. Here, one endeavors to be true to self and perspective, seeking to communicate truth in order to change and transform society. This is a *change-the-world* stage. As Fowler comments, "Stage 6 engages in spending and being spent for the transformation of present reality in the direction of a transcendent actuality." Many of those who reach this stage do lose self-comfort with respect to interaction in society and often become martyrs for their revolutionary, transforming cause or vision, since they are seen as subversives. But the people at this stage are not perfect; "Greatness of commitment and vision often coexists with great blind spots and limitations." This does not add to their acceptance and comfort. But they are highly committed and dedicated to their vision. Their eyes are fixed upon a kingdom wherein dwells universal truth, in hearts as well as society. Fowler does not believe that individuals seek this stage. He says "that persons who come to embody Universalizing faith are drawn into those patterns of commitment and leadership by the providence of God and the exigencies of history. It is as though they are selected by the great Blacksmith of history, heated in the fires of turmoil and

---

[77]Ibid., 184-188, 197-198, 200.

trouble and then hammered into usable shape on the hard anvil of conflict and struggle." It is the belief that God does communicate at times through revelation that gives impetus to a *radical monotheistic faith,* a term Fowler has gleaned from H. Richard Niebuhr. "Radical monotheism, in Niebuhr's usage, describes a form of faith in which the reality of God— transcendent and ever exceeding our grasp—exerts transforming and redeeming tension on the structures of our common life and faith." This occurs to an extent in stage six people, seen as their exhaustive commitment is active through their imperfection. In the Christian and Jewish faiths, one looks forward to an ultimate kingdom wherein dwells a unity and righteousness, called the Kingdom of God, traces of which are now present. This fact has been revealed through what Fowler calls the *absoluteness of the particular* in which "the structure and character of the ultimate conditions of existence are disclosed" through particular moments in history to particular people. As a result, Fowler calls the idea of the Kingdom of God a claim to absoluteness since it is the revelation of ultimate or *eschatological* reality. Although Fowler acknowledges that revelation is a partial expression of the absoluteness quality of God or the transcendence, it is only expressed in a limited manner through religious symbols and doctrines designed to convey it. "Now we see but a poor reflection as in a mirror" (1 Corinthians 13:12—NIV). However, it should be the human duty or "universal human vocation" to press into this kingdom, notes Fowler.[78] And Scripture agrees, "From the days of John the Baptist until now, the kingdom of heaven has been forcefully advancing, and forceful men lay hold of it" (Matthew 11:12— NIV). Stage six faith development individuals are involved in its advancement.

The truths of God or of the transcendent are universal, and God reveals and has revealed many of them at particular moments for humanity's benefit. Those that deal with the ultimate, future reality are considered absolute and a reflection of the absoluteness of God. Fowler sees this ultimate, future reality as a oneness with the transcendent and with all being.

---

[78]Ibid., 200-211.

In other words, all beings will be in unity with the transcendent God and with each other. This idea hints of areas in the New Age philosophy in which all are one with the universe and must look within to pull out the divine aspects already present and to begin to realize the unity toward which all are heading. However, the unity in New Age has to do with all that exists, not just human beings. The unity of all humans ultimately with God or the transcendent in the transformed kingdom is the philosophy of Universalism, possibly the reason for the name of this stage. Fowler's description of it, at first, appeared to deal with universal, eternal truth but then encompassed the idea of universal unity and oneness.[79] In the Christian concept, there is no *exclusivity* from the perspective that all who desire may enter the Kingdom of God (Revelation 22:17), providing they are redeemed from all unholiness.[80] Christ, himself, said he was the only way by which a person could be redeemed, "I am the way and the truth and the life. No one comes to the Father except through me" (John 14:6—NIV); because he "gave himself for us to redeem us from all wickedness and to purify for himself a people that are his very own, eager to do what is good" (Titus 2:14—NIV). This instruction appears to be in the realm of Fowler's *absoluteness of the particular*, being revealed by the one who rose from the dead, "in power and glory, as God's ratification of the truth for all people, of the proclaimed coming Kingdom of God."[81] The choice of the kingdom is the individual's choice, which all have the opportunity to make since, "The *grace* of God that brings salvation has appeared to all men" (Titus 2:11—NIV), and "God does speak—now one way, now another—though man may not perceive it. In a dream, in a vision of the night, when deep sleep falls on men as they slumber in their beds, he may speak in their ears and terrify them with warnings, to turn man from wrongdoing and keep him from pride, to preserve

---

[79] James Fowler, <u>Stages of Faith: The Psychology of Human Development and the Quest for Meaning</u>, 210-211.

[80] See Luke 13:28; 1 Corinthians 6:9-11; Revelation 21:8, 27; 22:14-17.

[81] James Fowler, <u>Stages of Faith: The Psychology of Human Development and the Quest for Meaning</u>, 206.

his soul from the pit, his life from perishing by the sword" (Job 33:14-18—NIV). Scripture speaks of the idea of choice often, and the Scriptures in Footnote 79 indicate not all will enter the eschatological Kingdom of God.

Universalizing faith pertaining to universal, eternal, and transcendent truth is a valid concept. However, the universality of all beings in a unified future in oneness with God in his ultimate kingdom has not been revealed through the *absoluteness of the particular* in Scripture, but the contrary is indicated therein.

Also, Fowler's concept of stage six in faith development seems to be more of a calling rather than a state of being.[82] The idea of total commitment without compromise seems valid, in which one's actions are consistent with the view of universal truth one holds. This state seems consistent with Erikson's last stage of Integrity, being true to what one believes. However, not all situations call for radical activists or revolutionaries. Some may have to suffer persecution, but it may be appropriate for others to be peacemakers. Stage six appears to be a valid stage, but it should be reworked into a state-of-being concept rather than a calling.[83]

The idea of faith is a basic human capacity or "calling" with potential for development therein being present at birth according to Fowler. He states, "that we human beings seem to have a generic vocation—a universal calling—to be related to the Ground of Being in a relationship of trust and loyalty."[84] This is what Fowler calls faith, trust in the transcendent God. Faith development, therefore, is part of human development and is dependent upon it. Physical growth and capability are necessary for cognitive thinking to progress and the cognitive development is necessary for social and moral development. All of these also are necessary for faith development, which involves knowing, perceiving, understanding and reasoning, socially, morally, and spiritually.

---

[82]See pages 48 to 50 herein.

[83]This will be discussed further in Part III.

[84]Ibid., 303.

Analysis

Just as a stage cannot be skipped in the developmental areas discussed in this paper, so also development in various human areas of being are necessary for the working of the whole. In a sense, it could be stated that human development should be holistic, the healthy working of every part for the benefit or wholeness of the total person.

The four physical stages of Freud indicate that a person develops physically which influences behavior and development. The four cognitive stages of Piaget set forth the mental reasoning process which contribute toward one's experience as it is perceived. The eight stages of Erikson set forth attitude development in relationship to society. Kohlberg's six moral stages show the growth of ethical perspectives. And Fowler and his six stages of faith convey the process of conceiving of and interacting with the transcendent God in a trust relationship.

On page fourteen herein, it was indicated that the areas of human development involve six categories, physical, emotional, mental, social, moral and spiritual. The major stage developmental theories deal with these areas. Freud's stages relate to the physical, Piaget's relate to the mental, Erikson's to the social, Kohlberg's to the moral, and Fowler's to the spiritual. An emotional development theory has not been discussed, however, it has not been left out. All the stage theories actually influence the emotional development. Emotions (as well as behavior) involve the physical and are subject to one's perspective of the environment and societal influence. One's mental reasoning capacities influence how one perceives the environment, and one's moral perspective influences a person's sense of justice which can affect emotions. The spiritual viewpoint has the potential to provide a calming, restful ingredient to emotions or the opposite if it is lacking. Although other theories have come alongside to contribute toward the conception of human development, the five which have been discussed are foundational and cover the six major areas involving growth.

Again, these life-stage areas of human development are not the total picture, but they do provide a conception of the complicated and involved process of this development. Understanding this process helps one to comprehend self in a greater way, to interact more wisely with others, and to enjoy life to a greater extent. This can contribute toward growth also.

In this life, growth does not have to stagnate or reach a plateau, except, of course, in the physical area which all too soon begins to deteriorate. In fact, growth and development should continue throughout one's life span since there is always more to learn than is possible in a million life times and since human beings, in this life, have not reached perfection. Also, generativity can continually provide new avenues of enrichment for self and others as one continues to grow and reach out to enhance and contribute toward the lives of others.

DEVELOPMENTAL INFLUENCE THEORIES

IV

There are various opinions on what actually influences human development. Some think it is all in the genes. Others believe the environment is the influence. And others assume that each individual person decides his or her own growth and its extent. As a result of studying the issue, influence appears to be triadic, involving the interaction of all three components. They may be referred to by other terms but mean the same in essence. Most common for the terminology of the first two of these is Nature (genetic) and Nurture (environmental). I would like to suggest that the third be called Notion (personal).

Although Freud viewed human development as being influenced mainly by "biologically based components of psychosexual development,"[85] Erikson acknowledged what he calls the three processes of organization. These he termed the body or *soma*, the ego synthesis or *psyche*, and "the communal process of the cultural organization of the interdependence of persons" or the *ethos*, all of which he

---

[85]Leonie Sugarman, <u>Life-Span Development: Concepts, Theories and Interventions</u>, 93.

considered necessary in understanding human action.[86] However, in his work he concentrated on the "social, cultural and historical determinants of personality development."[87] Another theorist on human development, Robert J. Havighurst, who specializes in Developmental Tasks, also considered the triadic nature of developmental influence. He calls these influential sources "physical maturation; cultural pressure (the expectations of society); and individual aspirations or values."[88] Besides the three basic sources referred to above, Fowler has included a few more in his perspective of faith development. They are time, experience (which he differentiates from nurture), and challenge, all of which he regards as necessary ingredients.[89]

Albert Bandura, a theorist in the area of social cognitive growth, goes into more detail concerning influential factors of human development with some cogent insight. His triad of sources is described by the following terms: "environmental events, personal factors, and behavior." Each of these areas has sub-areas which he considers. Overall, he views them as interacting and reciprocal, with the individual being able to make some choices which determine growth, motivation, actions, direction and destiny.[90]

Psychodynamic Theory

The first theory Bandura examines is the Psychodynamic Theory, which is the label placed upon the type of influence Freud set forth. It advocates the idea that a person's behavior is determined by inner drives, impulses, and instincts

---

[86]Erik Erikson, The Life Cycle Completed: A Review, 25-26 and 59.

[87]Leonie Sugarman, Life-Span Development: Concepts, Theories and Interventions, 93.

[88]Ibid., 94.

[89]James Fowler, Stages of Faith: The Psychology of Human Development and the Quest for Meaning, 114.

[90]Albert Bandura, Social Foundations of Thought and Action: A Social Cognitive Theory (Englewood Cliffs, NJ: Prentice-Hall, Inc., 1986), xi, 1.

which occur at the unconscious level (Nature). However, Bandura notes that people behave differently in diverse situations and circumstances. Therefore, they are able to temper or adjust their reactions to their environment. The Psychodynamic Theory is not able to explain this adaptive ability merely from the unidirectional, inner sources which, it seems, should provide consistent behavior in the individual. Consequently, Bandura does not believe the Psychodynamic Theory to be valid in explaining all of human behavior. He comments that this theory is not the most effective method to provide the expanded insight needed in order to help individuals change their behavior in a positive manner. To him, "The value of a theory is ultimately judged by its usefulness as evidenced by the power of the methods it yields to effect psychological changes."[91]

Trait Theory

Another theory which Bandura considers is the Trait Theory. It also focuses on the internal as a determinant for behavior (Nature), with an emphasis on a person's disposition. However, as in the Psychodynamic Theory, evidence for the Trait Theory does not uphold its one-sided claims. One's behavior should be consistent and stable according to this theory, but it is not. Also, it could appear that one would carry out every thought and that all actions would be the result of one's thoughts due to disposition.[92] As a result, there would be little self-control, wisdom, or learning from consequences. This theory is limited in its perspective.

Radical Behaviorism

Radical Behaviorism is the theory proposed by Skinner that there are two influences for behavior, Nature and Nurture, or the genes and environment. In order to influence

---

[91] Ibid., 4, 2-5.

[92] Ibid., 5-6, 11.

behavior, in this theory, the environment is the dominant factor which even regulates the inner realm of the individual. Therefore, stimuli from the environment are credited with programming an individual to act or behave in a certain manner. Stimuli also are seen to reinforce actions through repetition. This theory seems to make an individual subject to mechanical actions through external stimuli. According to Bandura, the use of repetitive stimuli is not as effective a method in influencing and developing behavioral capabilities as is the method of generating and operating cognitive tools. The idea of mechanical actions appears to bypass the thought process as well as the idea that an individual has some control over his or her actions.[93] This theory is limited in practical usefulness in explaining and influencing actions, considering the intricacies of human behavior.

Social Cognitive Theory

The social cognitive theory attributes behavior to the following triad of reciprocally acting factors: "behavior, cognitive and other personal factors, and environmental events." Here, Nature would be under the area of personal factors, Nurture would fall under environment, and Notion would involve behavior and cognitive and personal factors. This theory supports the idea that individuals have some influence on their own behavior, serving "as a reciprocally contributing influence to their own motivation and behavior within a system of reciprocal causation involving personal determinants, action, and environmental factors." Each factor is seen to influence the other factors in continuous interaction. However, their influence is dependent upon individual capabilities.[94]

---

[93]Ibid., 12, 14-15.
[94]Ibid., 12, 18-22.

<u>Basic Capabilities</u>

According to Bandura, the first capability through which influencing factors must work deals with the ability to use Symbols. The use of symbols enables the individual to adapt to and change his or her environment since they serve to convey meaning and give form to experiences which can be useful in conceptualizing and creating future potentialities and courses of action. Symbols are vehicles in the thought process and allow creativity.

The second capability is Forethought. Before people act, they think, making their behavior purposive and intentional. Thinking beforehand involves the use of symbols. People can think what the future might hold through the conceptual symbolic process and so base their actions accordingly. Thus, symbols are used in forethought which influences actions as their consequences are symbolically conceived in future eventualities.

Capability which is Vicarious is third. It considers the fact that learning can occur through observing the actions of others and their related consequences. Because there is much to learn, it would be impossible for everyone to reinvent the wheel and still accomplish their responsibilities. Therefore, it is necessary to benefit from what others have learned in order to be able to understand the essentials of our society today and to go on from there. Human beings have the capacity to learn vicariously because of the symbolic thought process.

The Self-Regulatory capability is fourth. This is the idea that individuals have the capacity to choose their own course of actions based upon their own standards and evaluative self-assessment or reaction to their own actions. This does not mean that there are no outside influences, but it does mean that individuals do exercise some control regarding their own behavior. They have the capacity to consider their actions and resultant consequences in light of their values and to make choices appropriately. It is obvious that symbols are useful here as one considers actions and their results before acting.

This capacity to consider one's own actions and consequences is Bandura's fifth capability, Self-Reflective. It is analytic and ponders self-consciousness in light of one's experiences. It involves self-appraisal as it enables one to gain knowledge about self and to evaluate one's thinking which affects actions. Here, symbols help in the analytic, reflective process.

All of these capabilities provide individuals with distinctly human characteristics according to Bandura with the use of symbols being foundational to visualization, thoughts and analyses. However, the extent of the capacity to use them as discussed above is dependent upon "psychological and physiological development."[95] Nonetheless, it is human to exercise the described capabilities.

Triadic Reciprocal Determinism

In the social cognitive theory, there is considered to be reciprocal interaction among the (already-stated) triad of behavior, cognitive and other personal factors, and environmental events. They each determine, produce or influence effects reciprocally, involving "mutual action between causal factors."[96] Bandura provides a visual diagram to conceptualize the interaction. It is produced as follows in Figure 3[97] with B representing Behavior, P representing Personal, and E representing Environment.

---

[95]Ibid., 22.
[96]Ibid., 23.
[97]Ibid., 24.

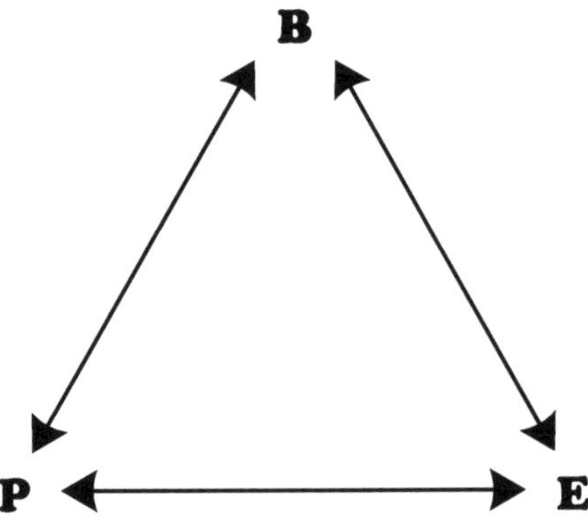

Figure 3: Triadic Reciprocal Interaction

Bandura clarifies reciprocality, indicating that the three factors are not symmetric in their relative, inter-dependent influence regarding strength, direction or time of influence. The reciprocality involves a great deal of complexity in interaction. Diverse activities, individuals and circumstances play a part in the interactive influence exerted by the factors. They do not act simultaneously on each other at all times; interactive and reciprocal influence takes time with the direction of influence varying. Also, the power of their interaction changes according to each individual situation. Reciprocal influences are determined somewhat by one's thoughts as to how an event or occurrence is viewed, the perceived meaning of an occurrence, and what is envisioned regarding future action or response as a result of the occurrence. Then the consequences of resultant behavior exert influence on thought processes. Also, behavior affects the environment which in turn affects how one thinks, which then affects future correlated behavior. As Bandura comments, "influences are altered by their reciprocal effects" and "counterinfluences undergo reciprocal adjustments during ongoing sequences of interactions."[98]

---

[98]Ibid., 30, 24-25, 27-29.

Bandura's social cognitive theory appears to provide the best insight into the intricate and complex subject of the influences of human development and behavior. This theory sees the factors as triadic within a reciprocally interacting process which varies considerably and is never the same due to different personalities, genetic makeup, circumstances, and environment.

Twins

It is interesting that Bandura and the other theorists discussed did not delve into the study of twins in order to understand influences upon human development and behavior. Twins are very interesting subjects, and they offer some help as well as provide some paradoxes regarding the issue of human functioning.

Even the study of identical twins verifies the concept that each individual person is unique. Although there are many similarities, there also are differences which contribute to individuality and distinction. In fact, even their fingerprints differ slightly although they have the same genetic makeup.[99] Also, identical twins do not always look perfectly alike even though they have identical genes. Their unique personality helps to distinguish them, though the differences may be slight.

With identical twins, the genetic factor provides a great deal of insight into its influence and that of environment upon development and behavior. And those identical twins who have been raised separately contribute to a greater extent. Researchers have discovered that separated identical twins have similar histories including illnesses at about the same time, school experiences, and participation in activities. Personalities, interests, abilities, intelligence, attitudes, body language and movements, mannerisms and expressive styles, thoughts, and development do seem to be the same or very

---

[99]Kay Cassill, <u>Twins: Nature's Amazing Mystery</u> (New York: Atheneum, 1982), 108.

similar as are the obvious identical physical characteristics.[100] Actually, those identical twins who have been reared separately appear to be more alike than those who have been raised together.[101] It may be that when they are raised together they strive for their own identity and that the interaction of experience with each other provides them opportunities for uniqueness. Those who have been reared separately may not struggle in the same way for identity; they can naturally be themselves without extra effort.

There is one aspect about identical twins that appears unexplainable. They seem to be in tune with each other without any kind of visible communication being present. Judge Charles S. Crail tells about a school experience with his identical twin brother Joe. Their teacher suspected them of cheating on their exams even though they were at opposite ends of the room. One day they were separated a further distance for an exam. Joe was placed in the principal's office while Charles remained in the classroom. However, at the time to begin writing the exam, Charles felt restrained and could not begin. As it turned out, Joe had not yet been given his exam in the principal's office. Once Joe received his exam and began writing, unknown to Charles but discovered later, Charles felt a release to write his exam at the same moment. The results of the two exams turned out to be identical with the same correct answers and the same wrong answers.[102] This ability is known as telepathy but cannot really be explained. It occurs with other identical twins also. One time when an identical twin was delivering a baby, her twin sister also had labor pains. Another time when an identical twin was

having a heart operation, the other had severe chest pains. Others are able to sense where the mate is though temporarily

---

[100]Ibid., 171-173, 180, 183, 185, 195, 225.

[101]Ibid., 190.

[102]Ibid., 160; Jay Ingram, <u>Twins</u> (New York: Simon & Schuster, Inc., 1988), 85.

separated.[103] The question is, why is this telepathy only or mainly found in identical twins?

It is known that genetic makeup is responsible for physical characteristics, and it also appears to be somewhat responsible for a person's disposition, etc. and how one responds to the environment. But what about telepathic communication? Does genetic makeup provide this ability, or does telepathic ability account for the similarities in identical twins with respect to personalities, interests, abilities, intelligence, attitudes, body language and movements, mannerisms and expressive styles, thoughts, and development? It appears that genetic makeup provides this telepathic ability among identical twins. With respect to other abilities and similarities researchers indicate that "every conceivable trait we've looked at turns up some genetic influence,"[104] but they also state that their "evidence does not exclude environment."[105] They note that neither the genes nor the environment work alone, but are complementary influences working together in human development with various levels of influence.[106]

Thus, the study of identical twins provides insight into human development. Genetic makeup, or Nature, is not the whole story of identity, but neither is the environment, or Nurture. They are complementary and interactive. Although the study of identical twins did not deal with the area of Notion, or the personal aspect of behavior, as an influential factor, nonetheless, this area which interacts with Nature and Nurture, reciprocally, is vitally involved, even with them. It appears more obvious when identical twins have been raised together, rather than separately, and try to assert their individuality and uniqueness so that they will be known for themselves rather than for their identical characteristics with

---

[103]Jay Ingram, <u>Twins</u> (New York: Simon & Schuster, Inc., 1988), 82, 87.

[104]Kay Cassill, <u>Twins: Nature's Amazing Mystery</u> (New York: Atheneum, 1982), 181.

[105]Ibid., 185.

[106]Ibid., 211.

their twin. They may try to act in a way which differs from their twin, and then others, the environment, will respond differently to them which will affect their thought process and self-image and self-reflection. It is evident, then, that the study of identical twins does substantiate the theory that Nature, Nurture, and Notion are all involved reciprocally and interactively in human development, though the degrees, direction, and time of influence vary.

Analysis

The triadic, reciprocally influencing factors of Nature, Nurture, and Notion do determine the thoughts, behavior, and thus the environment, as noted by Bandura in his social cognitive theory and as is evident in the study of identical twins. However, they work within an individual's capacity to receive and process their input. This relates them back to stage development with respect to the physical, emotional, mental, social, moral, and spiritual states and capacities of individuals. Yet, they are the factors which influence stage-development growth at the same time. Thus, it becomes obvious that the subject of human development is an intricate, complex, complicated, and elaborate arena of study. But if the attempt is not made, understanding does not advance and service toward helping one another is not as effective as it could be with more knowledgeable insight into behavior. Also, learning and growth contributes toward the advance-ment of society as a whole through which many benefit. As Bandura states, "human accomplishments result from the reciprocal influences of external circumstances, a host of personal determinants, including endowed potentialities, acquired competencies, reflective thought, and a high level of self-initiative"[107] evident in action. Thus, the idea of triadic reciprocal determinism, involving the influential factors of

---

[107] Albert Bandura, <u>Social Foundations of Thought and Action: A Social Cognitive Theory</u>, 41.

what can be termed Nature, Nurture, and Notion, appears to provide the most effective insight into the influences of human behavior and development.

IDENTITY

V

One is not born with a sense of identity but develops it as one becomes aware of self and is involved in relationships with others. In fact, as one grows and develops, realizing who one is, one's identity, becomes very important to the individual.

Meaning

The idea of meaning is also connected with the sense of identity. When one comes to realize a meaning and purpose for one's life and individuality, a sense of worth arises which helps to establish identity. Thus, meaning making plays an important part in identity as it attempts to make sense of the world and self. Meaning is not just information and the processing of information, but it deals with the why and wherefore of existence as it is perceived.

The idea of meaning is one which develops as one gains mental capacity with the ability to understand and reason and as one develops in social interaction, becoming aware of self and others. "Indeed," as Bandura indicates, "life would be most taxing and chaotic if people had no conceptions of themselves and the world around them. Their experiences would lack coherence."[108]   And as Erikson comments, "it is apparently one of the functions of the ego's unconscious work to integrate experience in such a way that the I is assured a certain centrality in the dimensions of being."[109]   Bruner agrees and states "that there is an ineluctably 'human' side to making sense."[110]   So, meaning is the organizing thread through which one relates to life and which in turn provides a basis for identity.

Individuality

However, the concepts of identity and meaning would lose their importance if all human beings were identical and if they were as robots. It is true that humans are identical in the sense that they belong to the human race and have much in common. However, each one also differs in many respects, and each one is an individual with a distinct personality and identity.

Choice

Although, as has been discussed, one's genetic makeup and environment are influential factors in the development of the person and the person's identity, the individual also has the capacity for freedom of thought, choice, and action. Therefore, the individual is vitally involved in what he or she is and will become. "The person, insofar as he [or she] *is* a real person, is his [or her] own main determinant. Every person is, in part, 'his [or her] own project' and makes himself [or herself]."[111]   But without the concept of choice by the individual, "the valuation of human dignity and

---

[108]Ibid., 36.

[109]Erik Erikson, <u>The Life Cycle Completed: A Review</u>, 89.

[110]Jerome Bruner, <u>Acts of Meaning</u> (Cambridge, MA: Harvard University Press, 1990), 55.

[111]Abraham H. Maslow, <u>Toward a Psychology of Being</u>, 2nd ed. (Princeton, NJ: D. Van Nostrand Company, Inc., 1968), 193.

accomplishments is diminished,"[112] and the individual feels worthless. In fact, too much conformity with little individuality and choice can lead to a sense of insignificance. "Conformity is one of the most fundamental dishonesties of all. When we reject our specialness, water down our God-given individuality and uniqueness, we begin to lose our freedom. The conformist is in no way a free man. He has to follow the herd."[113]

Therefore, it becomes important to realize the privilege and value of choice and of establishing individual identity and meaning; in fact, one seems to have an innate desire to do so. But the desire is that the meaning and identity be lasting and not temporal. As is noted in Ecclesiastes 3:11, referring to God's actions, "He has made everything beautiful in its time. He has also set eternity in the hearts of men" (NIV). "Eternity in the hearts of men" seems to indicate that human beings have a longing for eternal significance as well as eternal life. Therefore belief systems are important to individuals.

Belief Systems

Mankind does not want to be just a number or cog in the wheel of time that is here today and gone tomorrow. "Belief systems thus help to provide structure, direction, and purpose to life. . . . [They provide] personal identity and security"[114] (and some provide hope for an eternal future after physical death as well). Belief systems are relational. Fowler states that what one commits to is seen as having "an intrinsic excellence or worth and . . . promises to confer value on us. We value that which seems of transcendent worth and in relation to which our lives have worth." This helps to shape

---

[112]Albert Bandura, <u>Social Foundations of Thought and Action: A Social Cognitive Theory</u>, 41.

[113]Norman Vincent Peale, quoted in <u>The Reader's Digest Great Encyclopedic Dictionary</u>, s.v. "A Dictionary of Quotations: Conformist."

[114]Ibid, 36.

our identity and give meaning to our actions. "Our commitments and trusts shape our identities. They determine (and are determined by) the communities we join. In a real sense, we become part of that which we love and trust. 'Where your treasure is, there will your heart be also,' Jesus said."[115] Barbeau makes a similar statement, "It is the nature and quality of our commitments—to self and to others—which give direction and meaning to our lives."[116] Therefore, without commitments based upon values life appears meaningless. Maslow even comments, "The state of being without a system of values is psychopathogenic, we are learning. The human being needs a framework of values, a philosophy of life, a religion or religion-surrogate to live by and understand by, in about the same sense that he needs sunlight, calcium or love."[117]

Culture

Bruner comments that culture is a type of belief system which helps to provide shared meanings and values to its society and the individuals within it. In fact, the shared meanings and values govern the actions of those within the culture. Therefore, "culture and the quest for meaning within culture are the proper causes of human action," since "values inhere in commitment to 'ways of life,' and ways of life in their complex interaction constitute a culture."[118] Bruner notes that, although one does not always live up to the lifestyle of one's beliefs, on the other hand, commitment to a belief system may, at times, even override physical pain, "so powerful are the links to those meanings that give sense to life." Thus, meaning and values are critical and vital to individuality. "They become incorporated in one's self identify and, at the

---

[115]James Fowler, <u>Stages of Faith: The Psychology of Human Development and the Quest for Meaning</u>, 18.

[116]Clayton C. Barbeau, <u>Creative Marriage: The Middle Years</u> (New York: The Seabury Press, 1976), 31.

[117]Abraham H. Maslow, <u>Toward a Psychology of Being</u>, 202.

[118]Jerome Bruner, <u>Acts of Meaning</u>, 20, 29.

same time, they locate one in a culture."[119] Culture, then, with its values and meanings, can provide security and belonging but also the opportunity for uniqueness as one takes one's special place for the proper interaction of the whole.[120] However, if there is lack of meaning and value and significance, it is difficult to function advantageously and to contribute to wholesome interaction with others. But a healthy concept of self "is indispensable to becoming a full-fledged member of society."[121]

<u>Maslow - Hierarchy of Needs</u>

As one develops, so does a sense of self-identity. It is part of the human developmental process. Maslow has generated a concept of growth with respect to self and a hierarchy of needs.[122] It can be visualized in Figure 4.

Maslow's Hierarchy of Needs pertains to a perspective of self. As it develops in a healthy manner, growth is achieved in meaningful identity along the progression he sets forth. He sees the first and basic need as Physiological Well-Being, which involves "nourishment, rest and shelter." Complementary to this need is that of Safety, involving the feelings of security and stability. As the needs of Physiological Well-Being and Safety are realized, one then becomes aware of the need for Love and Belonging. This consists of a desire to have meaningful relationships in which one can both give and receive love. As this need is met, the need for Self-Esteem

---

[119]Ibid., 22, 29.

[120]In teaching, I often state that although a job or position can be replaced, an individual can never be replaced since each one is singular and shines forth uniquely, in a manner that no one else can duplicate. Knowing this can contribute to a feeling of worth. The following is a poem (quoted from Jessie Orton Jones, <u>Secrets</u> (New York: The Viking Press, 1945), VIII) which I learned as a five-year old that has helped my perspective of self:
> I am glad I'm who I am; I like to be myself.
> Even when I do the wrong thing, I know I am the right person.

[121]Ralph LaRossa and Maureen Milligan LaRossa, <u>Transition to Parent-hood: How Infants Change Families</u> (Beverly Hills: Sage Publications, 1981), 49.

[122]Leonie Sugarman, <u>Life-Span Development: Concepts, Theories and Interventions</u>, 30.

becomes important. This comprises the desire for a healthy view of self, self-respect, which consists of confidence in self, confidence in worth, and confidence in adequacy. Along with self-respect, should come respect and esteem for others. However, if one has little respect for self, it is unlikely that others will be respected. In fact, if one's needs are not met as one develops, the desire to fulfill those needs will be strong, and one may even be dominated by them.[123]

Figure 4: Maslow's Hierarchy of Needs

Maslow is noted for the last need listed at the pinnacle of his Hierarchy of Needs triangle. As needs are met, other needs become noticeable until they too are met. Finally, the Self-Actualization need surfaces. This need seems similar to Erikson's Generativity stage in which one is relatively content with self and desires to reach out to help others. Maslow defines it "as ongoing actualization of potentials, capacities and talents, as fulfillment of mission (or call, fate, destiny, or vocation), as a fuller knowledge of, and acceptance of, the person's own intrinsic nature, as an unceasing trend toward unity, integration or synergy within the person."[124] At this level, Maslow sees dichotomies dissolving and unities forming. One is not seen so much as self-centered or other-centered, but as fused into a "higher, superordinate unity.

---

[123]Ibid., 30-31.

[124]Abraham H. Maslow, <u>Toward a Psychology of Being</u>, 25.

Work tends to be the same as play; vocation and avocation become the same thing. When duty is pleasant and pleasure is fulfillment of duty, then they lose their separateness and oppositeness."[125]

The following characteristics[126] have been observed to be present in self-actualized people according to Maslow's perspective:

1. Superior perception of reality.
2. Increased acceptance of self, of others and of nature.
3. Increased spontaneity (spontaneous in behavior but will go along with conventional morés which are relatively unimportant but will defend what is deemed to be of vital concern based upon inner system of beliefs of fundamentally held principles).
4. Increase in problem-centering (rather than self-centering & often manifested in a life's mission).
5. Increased detachment and desire for privacy (emotionally self-sufficient and able to retain dignity in undignified situations).
6. Increased autonomy, and resistance to enculturation (independent and retain own values).
7. Greater freshness of appreciation, and richness of emotional reaction (enjoy life and appreciate blessings).
8. Higher frequency of peak experiences (transcendent experiences of ecstasy, wonder and awe).
9. Increased identification with the human species (love for and identification with others in spite of shortcomings).
10. Changed (the clinician would say, improved) interpersonal relations (fewer but deeper relationships with others).

---

[125] Ibid., 207.

[126] Ibid., 26; Leonie Sugarman, <u>Life-Span Development: Concepts, Theories and Interventions</u>, 31-34.

11. More democratic character structure (evaluate people by character, capacity and talent rather than status).

12. Definite moral standards (not situational ethics or expediency but the means to the end are important and should be ethical).

13. Philosophical sense of humor (not hurtful humor but educational humor).

14. Greatly increased creativeness (not bogged down, but free to be spontaneous yet efficient).

15. Certain changes in the value system or cultural transcendence (likely to show a calm concern with long-term cultural improvement than an active impatience or moment-to-moment discontent).

It appears from the characteristics of self-actualized people that they are alive and secure, basically content, knowing who they are and what they can contribute to the well-being of others. They are not considered to have reached a state of perfection, but they are balanced, wholesome and whole individuals. Thus, they are effective in their place in society. Their lives have meaning and purpose. They are secure in their identity, in who they are and in what they can contribute. Of course, their contentedness and security are not just based in the realities of the present or solely in this life, but in the realities of the future. They have "ideals, hopes, duties, tasks, plans, goals, unrealized potentials, mission, fate, destiny, etc."[127] (as well as eternity in view from some perspectives). But without hope or vision the people perish (Proverbs 29:18). "Hope deferred makes the heart sick, but a longing fulfilled is a tree of life" (Proverbs 13:12—NIV). "One for whom no future exists is reduced to the concrete, to hopelessness, to emptiness."[128] But self-actualized people

---

[127] Abraham H. Maslow, <u>Toward a Psychology of Being</u>, 214.
[128] Ibid.

have vision and hope, a reason for being, which can be conceptualized in future action.

Analysis

It is evident that identity is a complex matter, involving "past, present, and future time dimensions."[129] It cannot be conceived of in a holistic manner in the early stages of development because the cognitive capacity is limited. But as one progresses, the meaning and significance of the past and present can be analyzed with respect to self and significant future actions.

Individuals do not live in a vacuum. What they do affects themselves and others for good or bad. What they become does the same. What one does and becomes establishes and communicates one's concept of life's meaning, individually and socially. And one's identity contributes to or detracts from the good of society as a whole. According to Erikson's psychosocial development, "Identity is a way of expanding the concept of self to include social factors."[130] It becomes how one is known, what distinguishes one from another, what gives one significance. Developing identity is a continuing process throughout life, a continuing process in which one adds to it, revises and restructures it, and clarifies it as one progresses throughout life. There always is room for improvement, and the complexities of life provide the opportunities.

---

[129]Louis Breger, From Instinct to Identity: The Development of Personality, 330.

[130]Ibid, 329.

MATURITY

VI

As one increases in healthy development, more individuality becomes evident; and as one progresses, maturity develops. Maturity does not mean perfection, but it pertains to the idea of "ripeness; the state or quality of being fully grown"[131] or fully developed. However, a person may be mature or fully grown physically but not necessarily mentally, emotionally, socially, morally, or spiritually. Maturity in these other areas of development varies, but the mental physical capacity is a criterion for progression. To be mature in all areas is to be well-adjusted and to have wholeness of being with unique and meaningful identity. The definition of maturity proposed in this paper, as noted on pages eight and nine, is "the state of being wherein one has reached a balanced view of self and others, with actions reflecting concern for and interest in what is best for the welfare of others as well as society as a whole, without neglecting care of self."

Very few people are holistically mature, mature in all areas of being. Nonetheless, most adults (at least) have reached the capacity and have the ability to live uniquely meaningful lives which contribute to the effective functioning of society. Some continue to mature in one area or another throughout life, while others reach plateaus and cease to progress in various areas. Thus, their potential is stifled. However, those who continue to progress appear to have more satisfaction and fulfillment from life.

---

[131] American Heritage Dictionary, s.v. "Maturity."

Life Stage Areas

As has been noted, physical maturity and mental capacity are necessary for development in other areas of being. Physically, maturity is reached when one has stopped growing and the body is fully developed. Not all people are able to reproduce children due to various problems, consequently, the ability to have children is not a criterion for physical maturity. Physical maturity occurs sometime near the end of the Adolescent period of growth or near the beginning of Young Adulthood.

Cognitively, according to Piaget, maturity occurs when one is able to go beyond the concrete and literal modes of thought and attains the ability to think, reason, and visualize abstractly. When this type of abstract thought process becomes systematic and organized, it is considered to be mature. Usually, one reaches this cognitive maturity sometime during Adolescence.

Psychosocially, both of Erikson's seventh and eighth stages are mature stages. These stages are usually reached later in life, if at all. The seventh is Generativity with the virtue of Care. Here, what has made one's life meaningful is shared and passed along to others. Thus, there is a healthy perspective of self and others, involving caring and fruitfulness of life which enhances one's own meaning and fulfillment. Erikson comments that this idea is a "new version of the Golden Rule . . . Do to another what will advance the other's growth even as it advances your own."[132] A fully mature person usually tries to bring out the best in others and realizes a satisfaction as a result. Erikson's eighth stage is Integrity which leads to the virtue of Wisdom. If it is obtained, it is usually in Old Age. At this stage, one remains true to self and one's own values, accepting self and the dignity of one's life with contentment, knowing that it has been a fruitful and meaningful life shared with others. This involves understanding and discernment of life from a healthy perspective which contributes toward Wisdom. And this Wisdom can be lasting

---

[132]Erik Erikson, The Life Cycle Completed: A Review, 93.

as it is given to others. Erikson's stages seven and eight, thus, correspond with the definition of maturity given in this paper.

Kohlberg's sixth stage pertains to moral maturity which he labels as Conscience or Principled. This also is a stage which many do not attain, but if they do it is usually later in life. Here, one has a healthy respect for human life and dignity along with self-chosen, universally ethical principles to which one attempts to adhere. This stage is similar to Erikson's last stage of Integrity, being true to one's own values with accompanying concern for and sharing with others.

Fowler's last stage of faith development involves spiritual maturity. He calls it Universalizing faith. Very few attain this stage as Fowler sees it, but if they do it is often reached later in life. This stage corresponds closely to both Erikson's and Kohlberg's last stages. It also is based upon being true, without compromise, to universal and eternal truths as they are perceived. And it also has an outflow of respect and concern for others; however, it is more active, often seeking to change inequities and injustices in society, in a revolutionary manner if necessary.[133]

Maslow deals with the development of self with respect to the fulfillment of needs which leads to maturity. His fifth and last stage is Self-Actualization. Again, this stage is similar to the last stages of Erikson, Kohlberg, and Fowler. In this stage, individuals are content with self and fulfilled, using capacities and talents to help others. These self-actualized people know who they are, and they are secure therein. They have their own established identity which has meaning to themselves and is beneficial to others. They are fruitful, effective, and significant.

The concept of maturity seems to be similar in the stages of development which involve adulthood. These are Erikson's psychosocial, Kohlberg's moral, and Fowler's faith

---

[133]To be discussed further in Part II.

stages, as well as Maslow's needs stages involving self-identity development. And their concepts are similar to the idea of maturity presented at several places in this paper.

Not everyone reaches maturity in every aspect of their lives, but those who do, attain, not perfection, but wholeness of being. This is seen as a healthy view of self, based upon physical and cognitive capacities and abilities, with full development socially, morally, and spiritually, evident in behavior which benefits self and others.

Wisdom

Maturity also involves wisdom, which Erikson notes is the virtue of his last stage, Integrity. Wisdom in seen to be a practical virtue, especially in the biblical book of Proverbs which communicates keys to effective living, based upon God's ethical principles also communicated in Scripture. In Old Testament times, "wisdom was the practical ability to function successfully, to the best possible advantage, in one's chosen area of service."[134] This idea of wisdom is seen in Maslow's self-actualized person who uses or actualizes potentialities, abilities, and talents in fulfillment of a service or mission. Wisdom enables one to use one's life wisely as a result of the understanding and discernment of life's experiences. In fact, "the wise person is eager to learn from experiences and from the experiences of others."[135] The wise person is teachable, knowing there is always more which can be learned. But wisdom is not just understanding and discernment of life, it involves concomitant action, not merely thoughts and theory. Thus, it is practical. Wisdom is characteristic of a mature person, one who is balanced with respect to self, others, and life.

---

[134]Marvin R. Wilson, Our Father Abraham: Jewish Roots of the Christian Faith (Grand Rapids: William B. Eerdmans Publishing Company, 1989), 283.

[135]Stephen C. Evans, "Developing Wisdom in Christian Psychologists," Journal of Psychology and Theology, vol. 20, no 2 (1992), 113.

Analysis

True maturity, then, involves the attainment and enactment of wisdom through proper understanding of life's circumstances; physical maturity which provides the capacity for maturity in other areas of development; cognitive, psycho-social, moral, and spiritual maturity; as well as maturity of self and identity. This holistic maturity enhances the quality of life and makes it worth living no matter the circumstances. One is seen to be meaningful and important, not just for self but in relationship with others.

SUMMARY

Human development is an interesting study since it provides meaningful insight into the actions and behavior of human beings as they grow and develop. Problems are viewed as the result of deficiencies in development. But with better understanding, many problems can be overcome and positive growth and development encouraged. This is the reason for this writing.

Development varies with age as well as with area of growth. But it has been categorized by a number of theorists into life stages which involve sequential and necessary stages of development. Not everyone reaches all of the stages in all of the areas. In fact, few do. However, they give us a perspective of healthy growth into maturity.

First one needs physical development in order to have the capacity for development in other areas. Cognitive development also is important because it deals with how one thinks and reasons and views self, others and life. Upon these two foundations of physical and cognitive capacities, emotional, social, moral, and spiritual areas are able to develop. They are influenced by the factors of Nature, Nurture and Notion which interact reciprocally in the development of individuality and identity. As one grows, one becomes aware of self and others and establishes one's own identity. Maturity occurs as the result of healthy development.

Maturity, then, is the goal of human development. In holistic maturity, one has an established self-identity with which one is satisfied, and one's life has meaning and significance as it is lived among others and for their welfare as well as for one's own. From a mature outlook, life can be enjoyed and be purposeful. One can take one's rightful place in society, feeling secure and knowing that one can contribute to the working of the whole in a manner which is uniquely and identifiably one's own.

PART II

FAITH DEVELOPMENT

BACKGROUND

VII

Faith development is a subject which encourages one to think, especially in light of the criticism directed toward it. James W. Fowler developed the theory and first introduced it in 1974 in a series of guest lectures at Gammon Theological Seminary.[136] Since then he has published a number of articles and books dealing with the subject, the most popular being his book, Stages of Faith, published in 1981.[137]

Fowler certainly did his homework before setting forth his faith development theory, incorporating the contributions of H. Richard Niebuhr in theology, Jean Piaget in cognitive development, Erik Erikson in psychosocial development, and Lawrence Kohlberg in moral development. With the contribution of faith development, greater dimension is added to the field of human development in understanding the areas of human growth.

Before analyzing Fowler's theory, it is important to consider what Fowler attempts to accomplish with it. It appears that Fowler seeks to provide an understandable and describable structure within which he considers human beings operate as they seek meaning and purpose for life, longings or

---

[136]John McDargh, "Faith-Development Theory at Ten Years," Religious Studies Review, vol. 10, no. 4 (October 1984), 339.

[137]James Fowler, Stages of Faith: The Psychology of Human Development and the Quest for Meaning (San Francisco: HarperCollins Publishers, 1981).

desires which he considers to be innate within all human beings. He states that "faith development theory attempts to account for the operations of knowing, valuing and committing that underlie a persons's construal of self-other relations in the context of an explicitly or implicitly coherent image of an ultimate environment. Faith is understood dynamically as involving both the finding of and being found by meaning."[138] Thus faith involves meaning making in a social environment and involves the capacity to think, reason, and act. The capacity for imagination also is deemed to be important as it provides the ability to visualize meaning.[139] These capacities function together in the operations of knowing, valuing, committing, and acting as meaning is formulated. The growth of the capacity for meaning making is viewed by Fowler as faith development.[140] This links it with the other developmental disciplines. Since meaning making and the desire to make sense of one's life is seen as a basic human need and function[141] once a person obtains a capacity to think about life, Fowler's faith developmental theory provides an important area of study in its basic framework with which to view and attempt to understand this aspect of humanity. It is Fowler's desire that this understanding of faith developmental theory will "provide a criteriology for assessing the adequacy of a given person's or group's appropriation of its religious content tradition, and the adequacy of the tradition itself."[142] However, it does not require a religious inclination to function, since Fowler considers that capacity for faith development is part of human development and that the search for meaning is basic and universal whether or not one finds meaning for life in what religions may offer.

---

[138]James W. Fowler, "The Enlightenment and Faith Development Theory," Journal of Empirical Theology vol. 1, no. 1 (1988), 30.

[139]James W. Fowler, Stages of Faith: The Psychology of Human Development and the Quest for Meaning, 99.

[140]Ibid., *xiii.*

[141]Ibid., 4.

[142]James W. Fowler, "The Enlightenment and Faith Development Theory," Journal of Empirical Theology, 38.

APPRAISAL

VIII

Fowler's theory does not attempt to deal with religious content, which opens up his theory to some criticism. This is because faith is viewed by many people to have an object of focus. Thus, the need to define what Fowler means by faith becomes necessary. In so doing, it is important to keep in mind that words are only vehicles to communicate concepts. As long as meanings of words are understood there is no problem, but when they are ambiguous or when they have different meanings to different people, clarification is necessary.

Discussion of Faith

The dictionary definitions for faith are the following:

1. A confident belief in the truth, value, or trustworthiness of a person, idea, or thing.
2. Belief that does not rest on logical proof or material evidence.
3. Loyalty to a person or thing; allegiance: keeping faith with one's supporters.
4. a. Belief and trust in God.
    b. Religious conviction.

5. A system of religious beliefs.
6. A set of principles or beliefs.[143]

These definitions involve several ideas: trust or belief in something, being faithful to something, and believing something. Fowler's concept of faith allows for numbers one, two, and three, as meaning making involves "knowing (one), valuing (two), and committing (three)." However, he keeps his framework general in order to encompass all meaning making whether or not it is religious; therefore he does not deal with faith as content of beliefs as in definitions four, five, and six above.

From a scriptural viewpoint, faith is substantive and has an object. Hebrews 11:1 indicates that "faith is the substance of things hoped for, the evidence of things not seen {substance: or, ground, or, confidence}."[144] In other words, faith enables one to know that universal, eternal, unseen realities exist, and in the scriptural context, that God exists and can be trusted for this life and eternal life because he is the Transcendent One, the ultimate of perfection and ability. Actually, Hebrews 11:1 does not define faith as much as it shows what scriptural faith does. It "provides a platform for hope."[145] The following paraphrase of the verse helps in understanding its intent, "Faith through its active character gives substance to, that is, expresses the reality of, things hoped for; it demonstrates the truth of things not yet seen."[146]

Fowler's idea of faith in his stage developmental theory is not that far away from the scriptural discussion of faith in Hebrews 11:1. It provides a framework for meaning making which intends to embody universal and eternal realities which are intangible. Hebrews 11:1 faith also offers

---

[143]The American Heritage Dictionary, 1986 ed., s.v. "Faith."

[144]Logos Bible Software, version 1.6b. King James Version. Oak Harbor, WA: Logos Research Systems, Inc., 1993.

[145]Donald Guthrie, Tyndale New Testament Commentaries: Hebrews, vol. 15 (Grand Rapids, MI: William B. Eerdmans Publishing Company, 1983, 226.

[146]Donald A. Hagner, New International Biblical Commentary: Hebrews, vol. 14 (Peabody, MA: Hendrickson Publishers, 1990), 181.

meaning to life as it gives substance to universal and eternal realities. And both consequently provide hope which is reflected in one's life, hope that one's life counts and is meaningful both with respect to the present and to the eternal future (as is evident in Fowler's stage six perspective).[147]

Fowler's use of faith in his developmental theory offers a structure within which faith with respect to content can be analyzed. But if he tried to incorporate specific beliefs and content into his theory, it would not, by its limited perspective, be able to apply to the general nature of human development. Fowler "separates the content of faith (e.g. beliefs and values) from psychological factors that facilitate the operation of faith within the personality (e.g. cognitive, affective, and social development). . . . The way in which people construe and relate to transcendent realities is deter-mined by the receptivity and competence of psychological structures that underlie thinking, feeling, and social proc-esses." His theory of faith is operational and outlines "psychological prerequisites of faith development whatever the content."[148]

A New Paradigm

Because Fowler's theory brings a new perspective in understanding human development and because it deals with faith in unfamiliar methods, criticism has occurred. However, much of the criticism seems due to lack of understanding of what Fowler seeks to contribute in the comprehension of human beings. He does not nullify the content of faith or even types of faith but provides a framework within which content and types may be understood. He has provided a new para-digm in language and tools for insight which takes getting used to. They are conceptual.

---

[147]James W. Fowler, <u>Stages of Faith: The Psychology of Human Development and the Quest for Meaning</u>, 210-211.

[148]Marlene M. Jardine and Henning G. Viljoen, "Fowler's Theory of Faith Development: An Evaluative Discussion," <u>Religious Education</u> vol. 87, no. 1 (Winter 1992), 75.

> All science and not least pure science, is engaged in the construction of appropriate tools with which to shape knowledge and understanding of what is being investigated. . . . Really to get to know something we need to find the appropriate way in which to grasp it and shape what we grasp in our mind—that is to say, what we need are adequate modes of thought and speech. The need for conceptual tools of this kind is particularly pressing when we have to do with something radically new which we cannot understand by assimilating it into the framework of what we already know, and for which old patterns of thought and speech are not only inadequate but can prove quite false."[149]

New mental images and symbols are needed to perceive new discoveries. This is what Fowler has provided in his faith developmental theory.

Religion

Faith developmental theory provides structural stages through which people pass as they develop the capacity to make meaning of their lives. As noted above, it involves knowing, valuing, and committing to whatever makes sense and purpose to one's life as it is lived among others. Religion, on the other hand, is one of the entities which offers meaning. The dictionary has the following meaning for religion: "a. Belief in and reverence for a supernatural power recognized as the creator and governor of the universe. b. A particular integrated system of this expression: the Hindu religion."[150] Religion, thus, appears to be an avenue which provides for the expression of beliefs in which a transcendent power is seen to be the cause and sustainer of existence. However, some religions advocate the belief in many

---

[149]Thomas F. Torrance, <u>The Mediation of Christ</u> (Grand Rapids, MI: William B. Eerdmans Publishing Company, 1983), 16.

[150]<u>The American Heritage Dictionary</u>, s.v. "Religion."

transcendent powers, so the object(s) of religions vary. Because of belief in power(s) higher than humanity, religion is the most common vehicle through which to obtain and express meaning. Although some may consider hard work, fame, knowledge, pleasure, significant discoveries, teaching, etc. as avenues which make their lives meaningful, when the reality of death is considered, often it is religion, which contributes knowledge of the transcendent and hope for life after death, that provides real meaning and significance to present life. Religion has content—various beliefs and doctrine, object(s) of worship, symbolic rituals and liturgy, ethical codes to guide in daily living, and usually hope for the hereafter. Religion is the vehicle which most often provides the meat or body for the structure or capacity of the active process of faith, but religion is not faith. Failure to distinguish the difference between the two has caused some to misunderstand Fowler's work.[151]

<u>Types of Faith</u>

Another way to view faith is through types of faith, and because Fowler has not included them in his theory, some have difficulty accepting it. The following are some of the types: "'counterfeit' faith, 'authentic' faith, 'spurious' faith, 'imitation' faith, 'nominal' faith, 'passive' faith, 'sluggish' faith, 'intellectual' faith, 'sensual' faith, 'dead' faith, 'traditional' faith, 'demon' faith, 'heart' faith, 'spiritual' faith, 'vital' faith, 'transforming' faith, 'personal' faith, 'orthodox' faith, 'actual' faith, 'real' faith, 'obedient' faith, 'saving' faith, 'efficacious' faith."[152] Although these types are taken from an article regarding Christian faith, it is evident there are many types. Of course, the beliefs of a particular religion would determine the meaning and intent of various types of faith.

---

[151]John McDargh, "Faith-Development Theory at Ten Years," <u>Religious Studies Review</u>, vol. 10, no. 4 (October 1984), 340.

[152]Earl D. Radmacher, "First Response to 'Faith According to the Apostle James' by John F. MacArthur, Jr.," <u>Journal of the Evangelical Theological Society</u> vol. 33, no. 1 (March 1990), 37.

The bottom line would be, "Does an individual produce the type of faith advocated by one's own religious beliefs which should give meaning and sense to one's life?"[153] Fowler's faith development theory would help in analyzing a person's capacity for faith and present faith perspective. It would consider one's capacity for religious or meaning-making knowledge, values, and commitments.

<u>Action</u>

Beliefs, however, are not always consistent with or evident in action. But actions are usually true indicators of a person's heart. Fowler's theory can provide insight into understanding individuals and their "faith" or "meaning-making" actions because it analyzes people's faith perspectives.

Some do not consider faith as an action but as a gift from God. As a result, they have trouble with Fowler's theory because they see faith solely as a gift from God with no human interaction or achievement involved. To them, Fowler's concept of making faith a human act "undercuts the radical primacy of the gospel."[154] But the gospel is provided for all who will receive it according to Scripture.[155] And as Fowler indicates, God's prevenient grace makes acceptance of the gospel possible.[156] Fowler "has established the legitimacy and the necessity of studying the phenomenon of faith from its 'humanward side' as a process situated within the developmental history of the human person."[157] It appears obvious that people have a choice in their beliefs and in their faith or

---

[153]In other words, does one's faith reflect one's belief system in meaningful actions?

[154]William O. Avery, "A Lutheran Examines James W. Fowler," <u>Religious Education</u>, vol. 85, no. 1 (Winter 1990), 76.

[155]"Go into all the world and preach the good news [gospel] to all creation. Whoever believes and is baptized will be saved, but whoever does not believe will be condemned" (Mark 16:15-16—NIV).

[156]Ibid.

[157]John McDargh, "Faith-Development Theory at Ten Years," <u>Religious Studies Review</u>, 339.

what makes meaning to them. If there were no choice, and the gift of faith had no human input, all with God's gift of faith would most likely show evidence of it identically without error. But such is not the case. Actually, the idea of faith being solely a gift from God without contribution by individuals appears to be based on a misinterpretation of Ephesians 2:89 which states, "By grace you have been saved through faith, and this is not your own doing; it is the gift of God—not the result of works, so that no one may boast" (NRSV). Some take this passage to mean that faith is a gift of God. However, biblical scholars view the syntax as indicating that the availability of salvation is a gift by God's grace, rather than faith being the gift in this construction.[158] It is acknowledged though that faith can be a gift of God (Romans 12:3), but one must keep in mind that there is human interaction involved in this gift. Faith also is humanity's responsibility and is a necessary response on their part in order to receive the gift of salvation. H. Richard Niebuhr, a distinguished Yale theologian, saw faith in the same light as a human phenomenon, as well as a religious response. He considered it a human universal and a "constitutive dimension of human existence."[159] Therefore, there is basis to believe that human beings are involved in the faith process as Fowler so indicates.

Growth

Huebner of Yale Divinity School faults Fowler because he thinks he indicates that faith grows through stages,

---

[158]Francis Foulkes, <u>Tyndale New Testament Commentaries: Ephesians</u>, vol. 10, rev. ed. (Grand Rapids, MI: William B. Eerdmans Publishing Company, 1989), 84; Arthur G. Patzia, <u>New International Biblical Commentary: Ephesians, Colossians, Philemon</u>, vol. 10 (Peabody, MA: Hendrickson Publishers, 1990), 184-185; Albert Barnes, <u>Barnes' Notes: Ephesians, Philippians, Colossians</u>, ed. by Robert Frew (Grand Rapids, MI: Baker Book House, 1884-85), 42-43.

[159]Richard R. Osmer, "James W. Fowler and the Reformed Tradition: An Exercise in Theological Reflection in Religious Education," <u>Religious Education</u>, vol. 85, no. 1 (Winter 1990), 55; Robert H. King, Reviewer, "Review of <u>Faith on Earth: An Inquiry into the Structure of Human Faith</u>, by H. Richard Hiebuhr, edited by Richard R. Niebuhr," <u>Religious Studies Review</u>, vol. 17, no. 4 (October 1991), 293.

while he disagrees. To Huebner, faith is a factor which is present in all through God's grace, and while he admits it is related to "changes and emerging structures" of an individual, it, itself, does not grow but "becomes more and more a part of the complex evolving structures that involve us in the rest of the universe." Huebner's perspective of faith influences his approach. He considers it as a "clearing for God's presence," a remembering and openness toward God. As such, an individual ought to allow this clearing for God to become part of the other parts of one's "doing self," in other words, part of understanding, conceptualization, receiving, acting, thinking, feeling, judging, interaction with others, worship, and seeking God. One ought to allow more space for God, clear more space for him, according to Huebner. However, while he advocates that faith is a clearing for God which should be made larger, he states, on the other hand, that it does not grow. And at the same time, he says that it does grow in the following statement, "Growth in faith is not through teaching the Bible, but by making the Scripture part of the various and many facets of our life."[160] Huebner appears to be confused as he disagrees with Fowler. Fowler deals with the capacity for faith as one grows and develops which Huebner seems to admit is valid.[161] And the idea of making meaning of one's life does progress and grow from childhood through adulthood. The concepts of knowledge, values, and commitments do grow and change, and they are the basis for faith development in the meaning-making process. If Huebner better understood the premise of Fowler's theory, he would probably agree with it. As it is, he appears confused in his own thoughts. The idea of faith itself growing with respect to strength and complexity, rather than capacity of faith, is a matter regarding the content of faith and is best left to the perspective of a religious belief's point of view. Although Fowler does show how the faith and content of Christianity can be analyzed from his faith development theory, it is not

---

[160]Dwayne Huebner, "Christian Growth in Faith," <u>Religious Education</u>, vol. 81, no. 4 (Fall 1986), 514, 515, 517, 518, 519, 521.

[161]Ibid., 514.

based upon Christian beliefs but upon basic human nature, intrinsic to all of humanity, according to him.

Analysis

Some who criticize Fowler's faith developmental theory appear to misunderstand his perspective and purpose. He is merely providing a structural framework of humanity's basic capacity for faith, a capacity which grows and develops within individuals. This framework, thus, provides a tool within which to view and analyze the content and types of faith whether or not they are religious.

HOLISTIC APPROACH

IX

The faith element basic to human nature was not considered in the past in human development but is now being acknowledged as one of the ingredients in studying human beings holistically. It allows for the making sense of life which is a key driving force in each person.

Spiritual

The faith element in human development involving meaning making allows for the spiritual ingredient, since meaning making most often is discovered or accounted for in the spiritual realm. Technically, "spiritual" has the following definitions:

1. Of, relating to, consisting of, or having the nature of spirit; not tangible or material.
2. Of, concerned with, or affecting the soul.
3. Of, from, or pertaining to God; deific.
4. Of or belonging to a church or religion; sacred.
5. Pertaining to or having the nature of spirits; supernatural.[162]

---

[162]The American Heritage Dictionary, s.v. "Spiritual."

Many theologians consider human beings to be spiritual as well as material, attributing the fact of life to the spiritual life principle.[163] From this perspective, although an individual's material body may die, that individual's spirit is believed to live on in eternity. Scientifically, this idea can be explained by the first law of thermodynamics which is defined by Isaac Asimov as follows: "Energy can be transferred from one place to another, or transformed from one form to another, but it can be neither created nor destroyed." Asimov states that "no one knows *why* energy is conserved," but "all that anyone can say is that in over a century and a quarter of careful measurement scientists have never been able to point to a definite violation of energy conservation."[164] However, it is recognized that items can change from one form of existence into another, such as a log burning and changing from wood into ashes and gaseous vapor. Thus, there is the prospect for life after death, but possibly in another form such as spiritual without the temporal material as it is known today.

Since human beings appear to be spiritual as well as material and since it appears that there is a type of existence after death, it would seem natural to conclude that humanity has an innate inclination to discover or look into these areas. Scripture verifies this in Ecclesiastes 3:11 which states, "He [God] has also set eternity in the hearts of men" (NIV). This has to do with the idea of longing for the everlasting, the

---

[163]Merrill C. Tenney, General Editor, The Zondervan Pictorial Encyclopedia of the Bible, vol. 5 (Grand Rapids, MI: Zondervan Publishing House, 1976), s.v. "Spirit"; Walter A. Elwell, Editor, Evangelical Dictionary of Theology (Grand Rapids, MI: Baker Book House, 1984), s.v. "Spirit"; George Arthur Buttrick, Dictionary Editor, The Interpreter's Dictionary of the Bible: An Illustrated Encyclopedia, vol. 4 (Nashville, TN: Abingdon Press, 1962), s.v. "Spirit"; Henry C. Thiessen, Lectures in Systematic Theology, revised by Vernon D. Doerksen (Grand Rapids, MI: William B. Eerdmans Publishing Company, 1979), 160-161; H. Richard Niebuhr as quoted by Claude Welch, Reviewer, "Review of Faith on Earth: An Inquiry into the Structure of Human Faith, by H. Richard Hiebuhr, edited by Richard R. Niebuhr," Religious Studies Review, vol. 17, no. 4 (October 1991), 291.

[164]Isaac Asimov, "In the Game of Energy and Thermodynamics, You Can't Even Break Even," Smithsonian (June 1970), p. 6 as quoted by Henry M. Morris, The Biblical Basis for Modern Science (Grand Rapids, MI: Baker Book House, 1984), 187.

eternal, the spiritual. It appears natural for humanity to do so, and one of the avenues this search pursues is meaning making, making sense of life as it is in the present with the view of eternity in mind.

Meaning Making

People want to be significant; they want their lives to make sense and be meaningful, not just for themselves but for others and for eternity. Fowler's contribution toward under-standing human development incorporates meaning making into his perspective of faith as basic to all humanity. As he elaborates, "Faith is the patterning activity that orders our sense of the ultimate nature of the cosmos of being."[165] Among those who influenced Fowler in this concept are Wilfred Cantwell Smith and H. Richard Niebuhr who saw "faith as a dynamic, on-going, composing activity—the activity of meaning-making, the seeking of pattern and order in the chaos of disparate elements of lived experience."[166] As a human universal, Niebuhr believed faith, or as he called it "natural piety," was evident in all human beings as they "construct centers of value and meaning to which they give their trust and loyalty."[167] Fowler's contribution upon this perspective of faith as meaning making is his pioneering work of a faith developmental theory seen in developmental stages. And he considers this an intrinsic part of being human.

Whoopi Goldberg states she is involved in helping the homeless because she wants her life to count, to have mean-ing. She states, "I fear waking up one morning and finding out my life was all for nothing."[168] Therefore, she attempts to

---

[165] Sharon Parks, "Young Adult Faith Development: Teaching Is the Context of Theological Education," Religious Education, vol. 77, no. 6 (November-December 1982), 658.

[166] Ibid.

[167] Richard R. Osmer, "James W. Fowler and the Reformed Tradition: An Exercise in Theological Reflection in Religious Education," Religious Education, 55-56.

[168] Dotson Rader in *Parade*, quoted in Reader's Digest, "Personal Glimpses: Wildfire" (April 1993), 135.

find meaning to life in helping others less fortunate than herself.

Fred Rogers of *Mister Rogers' Neighborhood* also believes in meaning making. His program has been on television for twenty-five years and is the longest-running program on public television. One of his goals is to help children "make some kind of sense of what is going on in their world." He also recognizes that each child and person is unique and special. As children realize this, the fundamental seed of self-esteem is planted in them and can develop as they grow older.[169] Meaning making is important to children too as the popularity of Mr. Rogers testifies.

David R. Mason of John Carroll University discusses meaning making and connects it to faith as does Fowler. To him, faith is also intrinsic and implicit as "an attitude fundamental to the very act of being human." He comments as follows, also connecting faith, meaning making and the idea of eternity together:

> To be sure, many persons would not wish explicitly to affirm belief in God and some would positively deny it. And yet they, too, I believe, would affirm what we may call the common faith of humanity: given with human existence itself is the conviction that our very action, our every experience, is *something that matters*. But, if this conviction is so, then reflection discloses that no act, having registered itself in the world, can vanish into sheer nothingness; having occurred it has established itself as a value for all times. Thus every thought, deed, and experience makes an abiding difference in the universe; to be something that matters, is to be something that matters everlastingly. Therefore, I share Ogden's understanding that faith, in its most basic sense, is "an original confidence in the meaning and worth of life" or,

---

[169]Al Santoli, "I Like You Just The Way You Are," *Parade Magazine,* <u>The Sacramento Bee</u>, (March 28, 1993), 4-5.

alternatively, "our ineradicable confidence in the final worth of our existence." [Schubert M. Ogden, *The Reality of God and Other Essays* (New York: Harper and Row, 1996), pp. 34, 37.][170]

Along the idea of meaning making, Albert Camus once stated that there was really only one serious problem, "judging whether life is or is not worth living."[171] In fact, Mason quotes Camus who, although an advocate of nihilism, believed in making sense of existence:

> How can one limit oneself to the idea that nothing has sense and that we must despair of everything? Without going to the bottom of the matter, one can at least observe that in the same way that there is no absolute materialism, since merely in order to fashion this word it is already necessary to say that there is in the world something more than matter, there is no total nihilism. From the moment one says that all is non-sense, one expresses something which has sense.[172]

Therefore, Mason concludes "that to act in any fashion, whether to be creative of good or to be destructive, even suicidal, is to act as *if* that act had meaning and value in the universe. To exist at all is to affirm one's abiding worth— good or bad. . . . Each deed, no matter how seemingly trivial, is of unfading importance. Each experience, no matter how drenched in suffering, is seen to matter infinitely."[173] Thus, Mason agrees with Fowler with respect to the capacity of faith for meaning making as basic to human nature and as being

---

[170]David R. Mason, "Faith, Religion, and Theology," <u>Journal of Religious Studies</u>, vol. 15, nos. 1 & 2 (1989), 4-5.

[171]Melvin A. Kimble, "Aging and the Search for Meaning," <u>Journal of Religious Gerontology</u>, vol. 7, nos. 1 & 2 (1990), 111.

[172]Albert Camus, "The Riddle," *Atlantic Monthly* (June 1963), 85, quoted by David R. Mason, "Faith Religion, and Theology," <u>Journal of Religious Studies</u>, vol. 15, nos. 1-2 (1989), 5.

[173]David R. Mason, "Faith, Religion, and Theology," <u>Journal of Religious Studies</u>, vol. 15, nos. 1 & 2 (1989), 5.

important for individuals to consider because actions reflect meaning and individual worth and pertain to eternity.

Meaning making even is seen as a factor in well-being. In a recent article regarding a survey on the subject of happiness, it was concluded that "an important ingredient of well-being is a sense of meaning and purpose." People are seen to realize a sense of wholeness when they believe their lives matter and mean something.[174] This can be attributed to the meeting of humanity's basic need to seek meaning for life. As the theologian Paul Tillich noted, "Man is ultimately concerned about his being and his meaning."[175] In fact, it is considered to be a driving force present throughout one's life. Viktor Frankl saw it as humanity's "primary motivational force [present] throughout the life-cycle [and as a] universal human motive." And Ross Snyder considered meaning making or formation as "a central activity of the species 'Human Being.' The vitality—and graciousness—of a person's life depends upon their [sic] supply of meanings."[176]

The meaning people place upon their lives influences their behavior and gives their lives direction. In fact, in order to understand the actions of others, insight into how they perceive the meaning of their lives is helpful, as well as insight into their values and the nature of their commitments to self and others which also furnish direction and meaning.[177] Thus, it has been stated, "The best way to understand humans is to deal with the mentalistic meanings and values that occur in the minds of people, because that is the most direct cause of their behavior."[178]

---

[174]David G. Myers, "Who's Happy? Who's Not?" <u>Christianity Today</u>, vol. 36, no. 14 (November 23, 1992), 26.

[175]Paul Tillich, quoted by Melvin A. Kimble, "Aging and the Search for Meaning," <u>Journal of Religious Gerontology</u>, 126.

[176]Melvin A. Kimble, "Aging and the Search for Meaning," <u>Journal of Religious Gerontology</u>, 112, 114, 116.

[177]Clayton C. Barbeau, <u>Creative Marriage: The Middle Years</u> (New York: The Seabury Press, 1976), 31.

[178]Ralph LaRossa and Maureen Mulligan LaRossa, <u>Transition to Parenthood: How Infants Change Families</u> (Beverly Hills, CA: Sage Publications, 1981), 47.

It is natural for people to want to be significant and to make sense of their lives. Their actions indicate the meaning they place on their lives, and this helps others to understand them. Fowler attributes this desire for meaning and meaning making to humanity's basic, universal capacity for faith.

<u>Analysis</u>

When life is perceived as meaningful, a sense of well-being, wholeness, satisfaction, contentment, and happiness results. Meaningfulness is often found in the spiritual realm since human beings are considered to have a spiritual aspect to their lives involving the eternal. However, without a sense of meaning to one's life, often a sense of hopelessness, despair, emptiness, and depression results.[179] There appears to be no reason to live. But faith, which has found meaning to life, provides a reason to live and is considered to be the driving force and "the primary motivation of one's life."[180] Thus, Fowler is wise to include meaning making in a holistic approach to human development as an element to consider in ministering to others, especially in counseling and therapeutic work.

---

[179]Melvin A. Kimble, "Aging and the Search for Meaning," <u>Journal of Religious Gerontology</u>, 113.

[180]Charles W. Green and Cindy L. Hoffman, "Stages of Faith and Perceptions of Similar and Dissimilar Others," <u>Review of Religious Research</u>, vol. 30, no. 3 (March 1989), 246.

STRUCTURE

X

Fowler's structural approach to his faith developmental theory involves a personal theory of knowing and action. Meaning making is established through the ability or capacity of knowing, valuing, and committing which is seen through actions. In the structural-developmental theories (such as those of Piaget and Kohlberg), there is an epistemological emphasis which also works well in the structural faith developmental theory. According to Fowler, the structural approach to his faith developmental theory "has enabled us to find and describe structural features of faith that make comparisons possible across a wide range of 'content' differences. No less important, the structural focus has made it possible for us to systematically compare and contrast differing styles or stages of faith among persons who stand in the same faith community or content-tradition."[181] The structural approach is a holistic approach to the meaning making process and involves various cognitive capacities active in the knowing process: the capacities to think, imagine, interpret, reason, and judge.

---

[181] James W. Fowler, <u>Stages of Faith: The Psychology of Human Development and the Quest for Meaning</u>, 98, 99, 105.

<u>Stages</u>

In his structural approach, Fowler has proposed six stages of faith development which he considers to be invariant. In other words, they are sequential with each new stage incorporating and being based upon all of the previous stages.[182] Each stage is thought to indicate developmental differences in the operation of the integrated sets of knowing, valuing and committing and then acting. Fowler provides the following definition for his faith stages:

> Following Piaget and Kohlberg, we think of a stage as an integrated system of operations (structures) of thought and valuing which makes for an equilibrated constitutive-knowing of the person's relevant environment. A stage, as a "structural whole," is organismic, i.e., it is a dynamic unity constituted by internal connections among its differentiated aspects. In constructivist theories, successive stages are thought of as manifesting qualitative transformations issuing in more complex inner differentiations, more elaborate operations (operations upon operations), wider comprehensiveness, and greater overall flexibility of functioning.[183]

Fowler's stages evaluate seven operational aspects involved in his perspective of faith which are considered in each stage. They pertain to humanity's general orientation to reality and are listed as follows:

1. form of logic;
2. role-taking;
3. form of moral judgment;
4. bounds of social awareness;

---

[182]Ibid., 99-100.

[183]James W. Fowler, "Faith and the Structuring of Meaning," *Faith Development and Fowler*, p. 31, quoted by William O. Avery, "A Lutheran Examines James W. Fowler," <u>Religious Education</u>, vol. 85, no. 1 (Winter 1990), 74.

5. locus of authority;
6. form of world coherence; and
7. symbolic functioning.[184]

How one functions or operates in these seven areas determines one's faith stage, according to Fowler. Each faith stage is seen to provide a more dynamic and complex functioning in a predictable sequence of patterns. The pattern is believed to be universal and unvarying, but not everyone progress through all the stages; many reach a plateau in one of the stages and remain there. The chart of Fowler's faith stages can be seen in comparison with other stage developmental theories on page twenty-one herein.

<u>Pre-Stage</u>

The pre-stage of Fowler's faith stages is considered to be Undifferentiated Faith because it is a period of infancy in which the capacity for faith as meaning making is quite limited. Fowler also calls this period Primal Faith. He notes that trust forms are evident in this pre-language period as infants begin to form trust relationships with their parents or those who care for them.[185] This coincides with Erikson's first stage of his psychosocial development.

This infant stage is very meaningful to life-long spiritual development because it sets the foundation for trust in another. Early experiences of infants and toddlers are naturally more affective than cognitive. Total dependence upon a power beyond self in infancy prepares the child for interaction with others as well as for the concept of God. The "dialectic dance" of trust and mistrust leads to attachment and separation, a process of growth, which leads away from

---

[184]Romney M. Moseley, David Jarvis, and James W. Fowler, *Manual for Faith Development Research* (Atlanta: Center for Faith Development for the Chandler School of Theology, 1986), quoted by William O. Avery, "A Lutheran Examines James W. Fowler," <u>Religious Education</u>, vol. 85, no. 1 (Winter 1990), 74.

[185]James W. Fowler, "The Enlightenment and Faith Development Theory," <u>Journal of Empirical Theology</u>, vol. 1, no. 1 (1988), 30.

dependence upon imperfect caregivers and toward the concept of trust in the perfect God.[186] Although the concept of God pertains to content of faith, the fact is that this stage prepares the infant for the development of the spiritual. Also, because the infant is "inherently social from conception" and begins to interact with and trust others, this also prepares the infant for later involvement and participation in one's community.[187] Both the foundations for a spiritual perspective as well as social will provide a basis for meaning making in later stages.

<u>Stage One</u>

As the young child grows in the capacity to perceive and communicate, progression is made to the first stage of faith, Intuitive-Projective Faith. In this stage, there still is control by the parent but limited freedom and a sense of autonomy are introduced. Here, the child gains in the use of symbols, imagination, and gestures to formulate long-lasting images regarding the powers encompassing his or her life. Perception does not yet involve logical thinking but is gained through what is observed. Stories and visual impressions are influential at this stage in formulating thoughts and feelings and arrangement of experience into temporary and changing forms of meaningful units interspersed with fantasy. Also, the young child becomes aware of self and can only see the world from a self-centered perspective.[188]

At this first stage of faith, Fowler notes that the roots of ritualization begin. They occur as patterns in interaction are noticed by the young child. These patterns are termed RIGs which stands for Regularized Interactions which be-come Generalized. Often these RIGs or patterns become

---

[186]Donald Ratcliff, "Baby Faith: Infants, Toddlers, and Religion," <u>Religious Education</u>, vol. 87, no. 1 (Winter 1992), 117, 118, 120, 122, 125.

[187]Ibid., 123, 124.

[188]James W. Fowler, "The Enlightenment and Faith Development Theory," <u>Journal of Empirical Theology</u>, 30-31; Charles W. Green and Cindy L. Hoffman, "Stages of Faith and Perceptions of Similar and Dissimilar Others," <u>Review of Religious Research</u>, 246; James W. Fowler, <u>Stages of Faith: The Psychology of Human Development and the Quest for Meaning</u>, 133-134.

games such as Peek-a-Boo and Pat-a-Cake and then change into other games. What is important about these RIGs is that warm, nurturing interaction and bonding is developing with others, both children and adults.[189] The child, then, learns to communicate with others in positive relationships which provide a sense of belonging and help in a community-oriented association. This can lead to meaning making as one becomes significant with others.

This beginning of ritualization does not necessarily have a practical goal except as a means to express enjoyment and playful interaction with others. However, later in growth the RIG patterns are evident in religious liturgy. Some also believe that the religious rituals in liturgy do not have a practical purpose or goal but solely serve as a means of expression based upon the human need to spontaneously sym-bolize religious meaning.[190] However, religious liturgy and patterns appear to be more useful than merely to portray an innate desire for expression. They also serve to teach what is deemed important, are a constant reminder of what is deemed important, and reflect or provide an in-depth perception of meaning of what is deemed important.

Thus, patterns of playful interaction which begin in early childhood, form a foundation which enables the child later to participate in community relationships and find mean-ing in so doing. They also prepare the child to engage in ritual in a religious community and find meaning therein. This religious ritual can even begin at this stage in the form of simple prayers and songs of worship.

Stage Two

Transition to stage two of faith occurs as the child develops the capacity to think concretely and logically in a literal perspective. This stage is named Mythic-Literal Faith

---

[189]Mary Ann Fowlkes, "Roots of Ritual in Social Interactive Episodes During the First Three Years of Life: Implications for Bonding in the Faith Community," <u>Religious Education,</u> vol. 84, no. 3 (Summer 1989), 339-343.

[190]Ibid., 345.

and covers the period of school age childhood and beyond since some adults remain in this stage. Although stories are important here as in the previous stage, they are interpreted literally and in terms of reality rather than in terms of fantasy. Because of the literal and concrete interpretation, stories are considered only on the surface level rather than for their depth of meaning. What is not obvious is not perceived. However, they now serve as vehicles to communicate meaning to life as it is understood concretely. The world appears more orderly than it did in the first stage and the perception of others can be realized. Thus, the morés of the community are recognized and often applied literally.[191] This community recognition accounts for the name of this stage; the myths or morés of the community now are perceived with application from a literal perspective.

Since children and others in this stage think literally and concretely, they cannot perceive of abstract concepts. Thus, while they are exposed to stories, experiences, and concepts which contain abstractions, they will not understand them in a deeper sense until later, if at all. However, foundations can be laid for depth of understanding which can be delved into later and which can be a basis for further understanding. Therefore, it is important for adults to provide children at this stage positive, foundational material through their own lifestyles and actions.[192] These communicate meaning and whether fully understood or not, are observed and even copied if the adult's influence is positive and respected.

Stage Three

Synthetic-Conventional Faith is the name of stage three faith which usually begins in adolescence and for many

---

[191]James W. Fowler, "The Enlightenment and Faith Development Theory," Journal of Empirical Theology, 31; Charles W. Green and Cindy L. Hoffman, "Stages of Faith and Perceptions of Similar and Dissimilar Others," Review of Religious Research, 246-247.

[192]Delia Halverson, "Faith-Building Lifestyles: Enabling Teachers and Parents to Share Their Faith with Children and Youth," Religious Education, vol. 83, no. 4 (Fall 1988), 526.

adults remains as their faith stage. The ability to think formally in abstract concepts is necessary for transition to this stage because it is here that one begins to formulate formal thoughts regarding self, meaning and identity. As this occurs, one looks outward to find meaningful identity. Thus, the attachment to a group and others of like interests who are respected becomes important. These significant others exert a great deal of influence upon the impressionable people of this stage. Their formal operational thought has not developed to the point in which they are able to critically evaluate the beliefs and norms of those they revere, consequently, much of their motivation is conformity to the group with the desire to please the authority figures therein.[193] This stage corresponds to Erikson's psychosocial stage five of Identity versus Identity Confusion with the quality of Fidelity. Here, meaning is found in group identity which provides a sense of belonging. Authority also is found in others rather than self. Therefore, in the sense of belonging, there is a form of dependence upon the group; the perception of self and meaning is derived from identification with meaningful and significant others in group relationship. This uncritical acceptance of a group and its beliefs can lead to attitudes of idealism in which one's group is seen to be perfect and ideal and the basis upon which others are judged. Thus, judgmental attitudes can occur when others do not live up to a group's ideal. This can also cause a show of elitism at this stage.

The name attached to this stage reflects this conformity or conventional attitude and is synthetic because meaning is based upon the ideas of others without much evaluation on the individual's part. Nonetheless, as the individual attempts to make sense of his or her world, this stage

---

[193] James W. Fowler, "The Enlightenment and Faith Development Theory," <u>Journal of Empirical Theology</u>, 31; Charles W. Green and Cindy L. Hoffman, "Stages of Faith and Perceptions of Similar and Dissimilar Others," <u>Review of Religious Research</u>, 247; Sharon Parks, "Young Adult Faith Development: Teaching Is the Context of Theological Education," <u>Religious Education</u>, vol. 77, no. 6 (November-December 1982), 658-659.

provides a means of stability in the midst of physical and cognitive changes.

<u>Stage Four</u>

Fowler's fourth stage is called Individuative-Reflective Faith. It usually does not begin before young adulthood but may last throughout one's life. The ability to think critically and reflectively provides the basis for this stage. With this cognitive ability, attention or focus moves from the group to the authority of the self. The group is no longer taken for face value. Its beliefs and morés now are considered objectively but in light of one's own critical evaluation and reflective thought. The name of Individuative-Reflective Faith for this stage reflects the change in focus and critical, reflective thinking. One now assumes responsibility for beliefs and lifestyle involving commitments pertaining to one's new perspective of meaning and values. The world and others are not forgotten but are perceived through the conscious self.[194]

Meaning making at this stage involves a closer, objective look at symbols which were uncritically accepted in the past. Now they are analyzed and *demythologized*; in other words, the meanings the symbols represent are extracted and separated from them. The symbols may continue to be used, but now they are seen to be merely limited representations of what now is described explicitly through the vehicle of words. Symbols are viewed as tools devoid of the mystique they once had, while the words which describe their meaning take on value.

People in this stage have a coherent, orderly view of self and the world. They think critically and reflectively and are ready to take responsibility for their commitments and actions which portray their view of meaning for their lives.

---

[194]Ibid.

<u>Stage Five</u>

Conjunctive Faith is stage five faith. It begins usually in early mid-life if at all and occurs when one begins to realize that the world is more intricate and complicated than viewed from the orderly framework perspective of stage four faith. Stage five involves a mature outlook on life, not so much self-centered or other-centered as in stages four and three, but with a more open and balanced view of self and the world. Here, the views of others are not accepted at face value, but they are considered and analyzed for worth. It is realized that one does not have to agree with everything others believe in order to gain benefit from some of their ideas. Thus, there is a sense of interrelatedness in this stage with the awareness that there is always more to learn regarding truth and that others can contribute valuable insights in the learning process. One is not required to sacrifice one's own perspective of truth in order to gain benefit from the perceptions of others.

In this stage, besides a new look at the viewpoints of others, a new look at symbols is taken as well as a new look at the past. Symbols are not viewed mystically (stage three and before) or in a demythologized manner (stage four), but from an interrelated and unified perspective. Meanings are seen with their symbolic representations as a unified whole. Symbols now take on a new depth of meaning and enhance the understanding of the reality they represent. Their purpose is amplified. Also, the past is viewed in a new light with the attempt to recognize and integrate areas of value into the present, interrelated, multidimensional perspective of life involving self and the world.[195]

At this stage, the desire to share also is present. One finds significance in life in sharing what one has learned to be valuable and meaningful and what one has learned to be the purpose for life. Fowler comments that this "stage is ready to

---

[195]James W. Fowler, "The Enlightenment and Faith Development Theory," <u>Journal of Empirical Theology</u>, 31; Charles W. Green and Cindy L. Hoffman, "Stages of Faith and Perceptions of Similar and Dissimilar Others," <u>Review of Religious Research</u>, 247; also see comments in this KAM 2, Breadth Section, 38-39.

spend and be spent for the cause of conserving and cultivating the possibility of others' generating identity and meaning."[196] Thus, this stage is seen to incorporate the Generativity stage of Erikson which involves Care of others. Also, it includes the idea of maturity, which was previously discussed as "the state of being wherein one has reached a balanced view of self and others, with actions reflecting concern for and interest in what is best for the welfare of others as well as society as a whole, without neglecting care of self."[197]

Altruism then with the idea of passing along what has been learned in this life for the benefit of others is characteristic of this stage. Niebuhr would have agreed that this is a mature stage. His writings emphasized that human life is one of communal relationships with the ethical responsibility of care and concern for others. In fact he saw that "the beginning of self-understanding is the recognition of this fundamental condition" of communal interaction and responsibility.[198] David R. Mason of John Carroll University has similar thoughts. He indicated that a mature person's faith should be reflected in faithful actions toward others. Regarding faith, he states, "Being thus *freed from* the stultifying preoccupation with self or from idolatrous reliance on merely temporal goods, relations, or structures as the ultimate object of our trust, we are actually *freed for* responsible and productive living, for loving service to this world—to this world as itself the object of God's love."[199] Thus, one has a mature perspective of life in service to the Cause of all being as one serves and shares with others. In such a manner, one's faith can be seen to be alive and real. If it cannot be seen through actions, it is as if it were dead as James 2:17 (NIV) indicates, "faith by itself, if it is not accompanied by action, is dead."

---

[196]James W. Fowler, Stages of Faith: The Psychology of Human Development and the Quest for Meaning, 198.

[197]Pages 8 and 9.

[198]Robert H. King, "Review of Faith on Earth: An Inquiry into the Structure of Human Faith by H. Richard Niebuhr," Religious Studies Review, vol. 17, no. 4 (October 1991), 295.

[199]David R. Mason, "Faith, Religion, and Theology," Journal of Religious Studies, vol. 15, nos. 1 & 2 (1989), 6.

Mature faith, then, is reflected by appropriate actions in service to others.

This is not a static stage, but a growing and sharing stage, a stage of interest in the multidimensional aspects of truth and knowledge and, consequently, meaning for life. This is an "alive" stage with the awareness that there is meaningful input which can be gained and shared from self and others. It is a stage which reflects fruitfulness of life, both for self and others. It is a stage in which one is secure in one's faith, the meaning and purpose for life are realized, thus one is freed to act and share one's faith pertaining to meaning of life with others for their well-being.

Fowler does not view this stage as the ultimate in faith maturity. He sees some inconsistencies in it, since here individuals attempt to work within society and may, as a result, compromise and/or adapt their perception of truth. Fowler sees this attempt as an effort to maintain the status quo for the sake of peace and well-being rather than as an attempt to transform society with respect to truth as it is perceived. Therefore, his last faith stage serves to attempt transformation.

Stage Six

Stage six is Fowler's last stage of faith which is called Universalizing Faith. Very few adults reach this stage according to Fowler which can begin around middle age. It has similarities to Erikson's last psychosocial stage of Integrity versus Despair involving the quality of Wisdom, with integrity being evident as one remains true to what one believes. Characteristics of this stage of Erikson are seen in this last stage of Fowler involving the non-compromise of ideals and beliefs. However, Fowler believes that people in this stage are "called" to take on a radical, activist attitude toward society with the attempt to transform it based upon one's non-compromising perception of truth.[200] This truth is viewed as universal, being appreciated in various forms. The individual

---

[200]James W. Fowler, <u>Stages of Faith: The Psychology of Human Development and the Quest for Meaning</u>, 202.

at this stage attempts to embody this universal truth, as it is perceived, and to enter into "a oneness with the power of being" as well as a oneness with all beings who will eventually and eternally be in oneness with the transcendent Cause of being, according to Fowler.[201] Here, one is willing to expend all for the cause.

Fowler views this stage as more of a "calling" to revolutionary activism, however, than a state of being. Therefore, he sees very few who attain it, very few who are willing to give up comfort and spend almost all of their energy to transform society according to universal truth as they see it.

Fowler's stage six appears to contain some problems not evident in his previous stages of faith. He strays from his general framework of stage faith which can apply to all humanity and he seems to incorporate content and the calling of faith which are specific to individual beliefs and religions. Content of faith is seen in the idea of a universal oneness with all being irrespective of beliefs and action. This is called Universalism and also hints of New Age. Not all people and religions adhere to the idea, especially not Christianity which involves personal belief in and acceptance of the Redeemer who has atoned for sin as the only access to eternal life in the presence of God. The idea of Universalism seems out of place in a stage theory, which should provide a framework in which all religions should be able to analyze the particular characteristics of their contents and types of faith.

Also, the calling of faith seems inappropriate in a stage theory. Rather than a state of being, the calling to radical activism and revolutionary tactics pertains to methods and procedures, which can often do more harm than good. Transformation can occur through other means, in fact, the peaceful working within society through tactful and wise measures can accomplish a great deal. Radical, revolutionary measures are not the only way to transform society. There is a time and

---

[201] James W. Fowler, "The Enlightenment and Faith Development Theory," Journal of Empirical Theology, 32; Charles W. Green and Cindy L. Hoffman, "Stages of Faith and Perceptions of Similar and Dissimilar Others," Review of Religious Research, 247; James W. Fowler, Stages of Faith: The Psychology of Human Development and the Quest for Meaning, 210-211.

place for peaceful as well as activistic measures. But to indicate that activism is indicative of the last stage of faith is to misunderstand developmental stage structure.

Stage six of faith appears to be a valid stage, but the general state of being characteristics should be noted rather than content and calling of faith. Actually, stage six is not that different from stage five faith except possibly in four areas. The first pertains to the desire to transform society based upon the second which involves the acknowledgment of universal truth, valued for what it is although it may take shape in various patterns. The third is the idea of the non-compromise of truth. Here, one will maintain integrity although one may have to work through various measures to accomplish the transformation of society; but there is no compromise for the sake of convenience or comfort. And the fourth involves a sold out attitude toward what one believes accompanied by total commitment and energy devoted to the transforming of society.

In this stage, a higher level of stage five is evident. But while there is still the care and concern of others and the desire to offer meaningful service for the benefit of others, integrity is more evident in stage six. Thus, stage six shows maturity of faith. Perfection is not expected but integrity is. One's actions are true to character here and reflect how one views life and its meaning with total commitment in sharing the important truths one has learned to encourage, help, and bless others.

Analysis

The idea of a structured form for faith development is a helpful addition to the field of human development analysis. In fact, it is a very important contribution because it pertains to a framework in which the development of faith in the form of meaning making can be viewed. This subject of meaning making is basic to humanity and considered by some to be the motivating and driving force for behavior and action.

Fowler's faith developmental theory involving six stages of faith involves a holistic approach to the process of faith and meaning making as it incorporates the cognitive capabilities of Piaget and characteristics of the psychosocial stages of Erikson. But it adds further dimension providing a perspective for purpose and motivation which are realized through meaning making.

Fowler's six stages of faith development pertain to generalized stages which do not deal with contents or types of faith but with capabilities for faith. They involve universal states of being, at least the first five do, and stage six has been reworked to correspond to the same generalized pattern as the others. With these six stages of faith, meaning making from various perspectives and religions can be analyzed with the intent of providing helpful insight into the basic human desire for meaning, purpose and significance.

IDENTITY AND MATURITY

XI

Identity

Fowler provides for the concept of identity in his six stages of faith development. The idea of faith as meaning making incorporates the idea of identity because as individuals progress in gaining meaning they also progress in gaining identity. In fact, as they progress in age, individuals become more unique and thus more identifiable.[202]

Identity is closely related to meaning making which involves knowing, valuing, and committing and influences behavior and actions. People are known by their actions and these reflect the person. Scripture indicates the same idea with respect to words in Luke 6:45 (NIV), "The good man brings good things out of the good stored up in his heart, and the evil man brings evil things out of the evil stored up in his heart. For out of the overflow of his heart his mouth speaks." And Proverbs 23:7 (NKJV) states, "For as he [mankind] thinks in his heart, so is he." What a person thinks, then, is reflected in action. But what a person thinks is determined by a person's cognitive capacity. This will influence how a person perceives knowledge, values, and commitment and, thus, will

---

[202]Jon Rainbow, "Spiritual and Faith Development in the Later Years," <u>The Journal of the Faculty of the Southern Baptist Theological Seminary</u>, vol. 88, no. 3 (Summer 1991), 199.

influence a person's actions. These areas also influence how a person perceives meaning to life and one's individual significance; they all contribute toward how a person views self and one's unique place in the surrounding world. Therefore, as one develops in faith and meaning making, one also develops in a changing and growing identity. Faith as meaning making provides a reason for being. As growth occurs, the reason for being becomes individualized and, thus, identity becomes uniquely one's own.

Maturity

Fowler's six stages of faith development provide for the analysis of maturity as well as identity. Maturity is seen as a wise and healthy perspective of self and life in a wholeness of being, along with a healthy care and concern for others. It involves wisdom and the sharing of self with an attempt to generate or beget in others those concepts and ideas which one has determined to be meaningful, significant, and important. It involves the concepts and ideas which one believes will help others in their own journey or progress of meaning making.

In a sense, maturity involves the gift of one's unique self to others, not with the idea of pragmatic gain, nor in a selfish, self-centered way, but in healthy, life-giving service with the desire that one's contribution will take fruit in others also for their benefit and wholeness of being.

SUMMARY

James Fowler has made a valuable contribution to the field of human development by introducing a new concept of faith theory involving developmental stages pertaining to meaning making, which is a basic and universal desire of humanity. This provides for a holistic approach to human development since it corresponds with other developmental theories and contributes toward the understanding of human growth.

Fowler does not attempt to deal with the content or types of individual faith but with the basic structural capacity for faith so that individual faith can be analyzed with respect to content, types and maturity. Many who criticize Fowler misunderstand his purpose and the benefits which his theory can provide to their individual faith perspectives. Fowler presents a new paradigm with an unfamiliar method of viewing faith. But it provides a helpful tool for analysis of humanity's basic capacity for faith which seeks to provide meaning for life.

Fowler's faith theory involves six developmental stages which are considered to be invariant and sequential although not everyone progresses through all stages. Each succeeding stage is viewed to be more complex and dynamic than the previous stages which are foundational to those above. They also are viewed as universal and unvarying and correspond to Piaget's cognitive stages and Erikson's psycho-social stages of development but add the new dimension of faith as meaning making. In each stage, seven operational aspects are evaluated with respect to one's general orientation to reality. How one functions or responds to these operational aspects determines the faith stage in which one operates.

Identity is connected with Fowler's faith theory since his theory provides a structure in which meaning making is developed, and meaning making provides for identity. Thus, the forming of one's identity is deemed to be a developmental process and is reflected in actions which portray thoughts. Thoughts involve perception of knowledge, values and direction for commitment. As the capacity for cognitive thinking develops, so does the capacity for meaning making and thus identity. Meaning provides significance and a reason for being; this developed reason for being becomes uniquely one's own as it is cultivated and refined through the developmental process. This reason for being is how one views self and is reflected in relevant actions. The reason for being, then, provides one's unique identity. It is connected with the faith developmental process.

Fowler's faith developmental theory also provides for the analysis of maturity. It pertains to wholeness of being and is seen in the last two stages of faith development. These stages emphasize care and concern for others with the desire to share from one's life what is deemed to be meaningful in the hopes that it will generate or produce benefit in the lives of others. Sharing enhances and contributes toward meaning and significance to one's life. Consequently, in maturity one's life is active in meaning making, both for self and others.

The faith developmental theory of James Fowler, as it incorporates meaning making along with the forming of identity and maturity, is of tremendous benefit in the study of human growth. It covers areas which are basic to humanity and which are motivational forces seen in behavior and action. His theory is a needed and valuable addition in understanding humanity.

PART III

FAITH STAGE DEVELOPMENT IN SCRIPTURE

The stages of faith development proposed by James Fowler provide a framework within which to analyze the growth and development of the capacity for faith in Israel and the Church. This analysis is viewed with the backdrop of God's interaction with His people and their interaction with Him and others as recorded in Scripture. For visual understanding, Figure 5 is provided, using Piaget's cognitive stages, Erikson's psycho-social stages, and Fowler's faith stages along with the faith stages of God's people as seen scripturally. These are referred to as the biblical journey stages.

Intrinsic with stage developmental models are the following features characteristic of the structures:

1. The stages are sequential;
2. Each stage is necessary before arrival at a succeeding stage;
3. Each succeeding stage is more intricate and represents a stage development in a new form; and
4. Each stage is foundational and preparatory for the next succeeding stage.[203]

Also, the cognitive process is essential to stage development and is considered in Fowler's faith developmental theory. It involves a person going "from an undifferentiated state of sensations and reflexes; to a physical (sensorimotor)

---

[203] Adapted from Louis Breger, From Instinct to Identity: The Development of Personality, 9.

LIFE-STAGE AGES		PIAGET'S COGNITIVE STAGES 	ERIKSON'S PSYCHO-SOCIAL STAGES 	FOWLER'S FAITH STAGES 	BIBLICAL JOURNEY STAGES 
Infancy Birth thru 1 Year		1 Sensori-motor	1 Trust	Undifferentiated Faith	Birth of Israel, Exodus, Wilderness
Early Child-hood 2 thru 3 Years		2 Preoper-ational Thinking, Basic Symbolism	2 Autonomy	1 Intuitive-Projective Faith	1 Crossing Jordan, Conquest, Period of Judges
Play Age 4 thru 5 Years			3 Initiative		
School Age 6 thru 11 Years		3 Concrete, Literal Thought	4 Industry	2 Mythic-Literal Faith	2 Monarchy (United & Divided)
Adoles-cence 12 to 18 Years		4 Formal, Abstract Thought	5 Identity	3 Synthetic-Conventional Faith	3 Exile, Return, Silence
Young Adult-hood 18 to 35 Years			6 Intimacy	4 Individuative-Reflective Faith	4 Birth of the Church
Adult-hood 35 to 65 Years			7 Generativity	5 Conjunctive Faith	5 Witnessing Church
Old Age 65+ Years			8 Integrity	6 Universalizing Faith	6 Serving & Sold-Out Church

**Figure 5: Areas of Developmental Life Stages
with Biblical Journey Stages**

apprehension of self and the world; to crude symbolic (intuitive) categories; to a more differentiated—but still literal or concrete—mode of thought to, finally, the ability to manipulate abstractions."[204]   Thus, a person's cognitive ability influences perception of self and the surrounding world. This is verified in "interview after interview with children [which] repeatedly reinforces the fact that at certain stages things are seen from a perspective which is significantly different from an earlier or later perspective."[205]   In fact, the younger a person is, the more simple is the perception of self and the world than in an older person.[206]

Psychosocial stages are included in Figure 5 for comparison with cognitive and faith stages since social growth also corresponds with cognitive and faith growth in human development. In fact, the patterns and characteristics of social development are seen to relate closely with those of faith development.

Although Israel and the Church are nations or organizations, their constituents are people who did or do grow, change and develop. But even laying aside the human aspect, Israel and the Church, as entities, appear to have developed along the stages of faith parameters set forth by Fowler.

---

[204]Ibid.

[205]Ronald Duska and Mariellen Whelan, <u>Moral Development: A Guide to Piaget and Kohlberg</u> (New York: Paulist Press, 1975), 7.

[206]Kurt Lewin, <u>A Dynamic Theory of Personality: Selected Papers</u>, trans. by Donald K. Adams and Karl E. Zener (New York: McGraw-Hill Book Company, Inc., 1935), 187.

PREPARATION

XII

Before Israel could become a nation with the evidence of faith stages, preparation was involved. Therefore, the topics of conception, prenatal development, and birth are discussed first before the faith stages.

<u>Conception</u>

Israel was conceived when Abraham responded in faith to God's intervention in his life. God had chosen to work through a group of people to make Himself known to the world. As Abraham responded positively to God in faith, God chose Abraham and his descendants as the people through whom He would work. This does not mean that God did not work through anyone else. He did. Scripture records Melchizedek and Job, specifically, who served Him during the general patriarchal time frame of Abraham. However, God also chose to work through a people, who would become a nationality, to be His authorized representatives. The following account from Genesis 12:1-4 (NIV) records God's interaction with Abraham and his response:

The LORD had said to Abram, "Leave your country, your people and your father's household and go to the land I will show you.

I will make you into a great nation
and I will bless you;
I will make your name great,
and you will be a blessing.
I will bless those who bless you,
and whoever curses you I will curse;
and all peoples on earth will be blessed through you."

So Abram left, as the LORD had told him.

Because of Abraham's obedience, God conceived through him a group of people through whom He would work. Abraham's obedience because of faith and trust in God was attributed to him as righteousness (Gen. 15:6). At later times, God confirmed this promise to Abraham and others, adding more detail,[207] but already at conception were the ideas of a land, a great nation, a great name for Abraham, and a blessing to all other peoples. Even at this beginning stage, the priestly aspect of drawing others to God's blessing and Abraham's people also receiving blessing is evident. However, obedience was required as it was of Abraham (Gen. 17:9; 18:19).

Prenatal Development

Prenatal development of Israel was slow and lengthy. At the conception, so to speak, of the nation of Israel, Abraham was married but had no children. God performed a miracle, and twenty-five years after God had first dealt with Abraham (as far as is recorded), a son, Isaac, was born to Abraham and Sarah through God's supernatural enabling. Now there was one official descendant to contribute toward the makeup of the nation under Abraham which would be Israel. However, it was not until forty years of age that Isaac married, and then only through prayer to God and a miracle did children come twenty years later. Actually, twins were born, but the coming nation was to go through the younger of

---

[207]See Genesis 15:5-6, 18-21; 17:4-8, 15-19; 18:18; 21:12; 22:17-18; 26:4-5; 28:4, 14-15.

the two, Jacob, rather than the firstborn, Esau. Later Jacob was renamed Israel by God, thus the name of the eventual nation. Israel means, "God prevails,"[208] and He did prevail in Jacob/Israel's life at Peniel. Again, the process was slow. Jacob did not marry until probably his early eighties, but then the speed picked up. Jacob had twelve sons who became known as the twelve tribes of Israel. They began to multiply by marrying women in the land of Canaan, and the possibility existed that they would adapt to the religious ways of the people of Canaan. Consequently, God provided an incubator-type of environment for them in which to grow and yet retain their spiritual identity, preparing them for their nationhood which could represent Him to the world. He provided a location in the land of Goshen in Egypt. It was a fertile land appropriate for their sheep, and it was somewhat removed from the Egyptians who did not care for sheep and shepherds. When Jacob and his descendants entered Egypt, there were seventy-five of them, not counting Jacob's son's wives but including Jacob and Joseph's family of four (Genesis 46:26-27; Exodus 1:5; Acts 7:14). Although there was some inter-mingling, overall, the descendants of Jacob/Israel retained their identity and did not assimilate into the Egyptian culture. In Egypt, these people grew in number and strength, and after about four hundred years in Egypt (Genesis 15:13; Acts 7:6), they were about ready to become a nation.

Overall, the prenatal stage lasted about six hundred and fifteen years. By then, Abraham's descendants through Isaac and Jacob numbered around 603,550 men who were twenty years of age and older, besides the women and children (Exodus 38:26). They were a people ready for birth.

Birth

Birth of the nation of Israel occurred at the miraculous Exodus from Egypt. In a sense it was birth through water, the water of the Red (actually Reed) Sea. It was then that the Israelites became an independent people under their God who

---

[208]Logos Bible Software, version 1.6b, s.v. "Israel."

delivered them (Exodus 18:8; 29:46; Deuteronomy 4:20), who gave them birth. Terminology in Isaiah 46:3 (NKJV) refers to God's involvement in the birth of Israel. Israel is mentioned as those "who have been upheld by Me [God] from birth, Who have been carried from the womb." In fact, the essence of Jeremiah 2:27 indicates that God is the Father of Israel and responsible for their birth but that Israel, at the time of Jeremiah, did not acknowledge it.

Signifying that the exodus signaled Israel's birth and a beginning, God gave the Israelites a new calendar at that time. The beginning of each new year would be at the beginning of the month in which they left Egypt according to Exodus 12:1-2, "The LORD said to Moses and Aaron in the land of Egypt: This month shall mark for you the beginning of months; it shall be the first month of the year for you."

Thus, the nation of Israel was officially born. The Israelites became a substantial group of people in their own right at the exodus. From this period on in their biblical history, their faith capacity and development can be analyzed.

FAITH STAGES

XIII

James Fowler proposes six actual faith stages which are included in his theory of development. Although the first period is not an actual stage, Fowler calls it a pre-stage which occurs immediately after birth and through the first year. He calls this stage Undifferentiated Faith.

Pre-Stage

According to Fowler, Undifferentiated Faith which occurs in infancy through one year as a pre-stage is quite limited with respect to meaning making. But it is a critical period in which trust relationships are formed. With respect to Israel, in the pre-stage, the nation was exposed to a trust relationship with God as the parental Father.

The nation had just been birthed. The people had been slaves and had no concept of how to organize themselves as a nation or how to act on their own independently. There were no experienced leaders among them except for Moses, and he had been tending his father-in-law's sheep for the past forty years and out of touch with leadership responsibilities received in his upbringing as the adopted son of Pharaoh's daughter. They were babies, so to speak, and God took them gently by the hand and guided them every step of the way in their new journey into independent life.

TABERNACLE GOD REVEALED TO MOSES

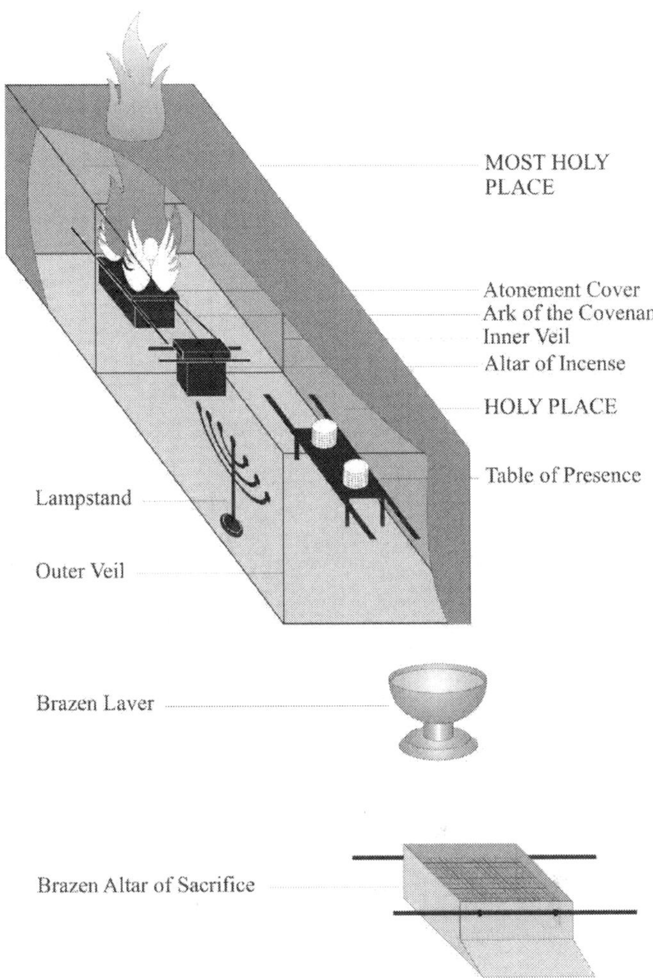

SYMBOLIC APPROACH TO THE HOLY GOD

Figure 6: Old Testament Tabernacle Layout

It was difficult for the Israelites to trust God since they had found by experience that they could not trust their Egyptian taskmasters. The Israelites murmured and grumbled a lot, as babies crying to have their needs met. But God was always there for them, guiding them and providing water and *manna* or "pablum" miraculously and giving them victory over their enemies whom they encountered in their new journey. The whole time during the forty years in the wilderness neither their clothes nor their shoes wore out (Deuteronomy 29:5); God totally provided for them as a patient, faithful Father. Because He had created and birthed them, He knew they did not know how to care for themselves at first.

Even in their infancy, God provided Israel with symbolic imagery. They were not expected to understand the meanings but to get used to and familiar with the pictures. Eventually, as they grew, the pictures would take on significance. But God taught them gradually.

The main pictures God provided involved the Tabernacle and ritualistic worship of God seen in daily life and on special commemorative days throughout the year. Although God was not to be visualized tangibly, lest the people make false idols as did the surrounding nations, He made His presence known through the symbolic, intangible pillar of cloud and fire which emanated from the midst of the Mercy Seat in the Most Holy Place of the Tabernacle.

The Tabernacle and its accompanying articles and ritualistic procedures portrayed approach to the most holy God (see Figure 6). First of all, the people had to be cleansed through the blood sacrifice made at the Bronze Altar. Between the Altar and the Tabernacle was the Bronze Laver which signified the cleansing which led to the availability of the provisions inside the Tabernacle. The first room inside the Tabernacle was the Holy Place. Therein were found the Golden Lampstand and the Table of Shewbread (or Presence) as well as the Altar of Incense. The Lampstand signified the light of the presence of the Lord to guide His people. The Table of Shewbread signified the bread of life which the Lord provides as well as table fellowship, enjoying the presence of the Lord and His sustenance. And the Altar of Incense represented the prayers of God's people. Between the Holy Place and the Most Holy Place was a heavy veil separating the two rooms. This separation was necessary because God's holy, symbolic presence was represented in the Most Holy Place. No one could enter there and remain alive except the High Priest, and only he could remain alive if he entered once a year on the Day of Atonement and followed procedures properly.

All this showed that a mediator was necessary for the people to have access to their God, but access was only through the symbolic cleansing power of the blood of animals. However, God did dwell among His people, as a father with His children. Awareness of His presence was constantly seen in the midst of them. This was to be encouraging and a factor to build their infant trust in Him. Understanding of the ritual would come later.

Also in their infant stage, God provided a basic moral code called the Ten Commandments. These commandments were to be the constitution of the newly formed nation and contained a generalized framework of moral responsibility, vertically toward God (the first four commandments) and horizontally toward humanity (the last six commandments). This moral code is still considered as the basic outline of responsibility toward others in most cultures. Even the responsibility toward God is considered accurate from a Christian perspective today. The Ten Commandments are found in Exodus 20 and are summarized and paraphrased as follows:

1. Worship only the one, true God;
2. Do not create idols to worship;
3. Do not swear against the Lord;
4. Worship once a week on the Sabbath (the Lord's day);
5. Honor father and mother;
6. Do not kill (murder);
7. Do not commit adultery;

8.   Do not steal;

9.   Do not gossip or bear false witness; and

10.   Do not covet what another has.

Later in this pre-stage, God emphasized the first commandment, stating in Deuteronomy 6:4-5 (KJV) that He was one God, "Hear, O Israel: The LORD our God is one LORD. And thou shalt love the LORD thy God with all thine heart, and with all thy soul, and with all thy might." God emphasized that He was one God because the nations the Israelites would soon come in contact with those who worshipped many other gods. But they were to be separate from them and worship and represent Him alone. At first in their history and then much later, they would adhere to this elaboration of the first commandment, and later Deuteronomy 6:4 would become a very important statement for them. However, there were periods in their developmental stages when they would test their wings and go far from God as they worshipped others.

Actually hidden within Deuteronomy 6:4 is the idea of plurality of persons in the one God. But the Israelites were not yet ready for this unveiling of truth because they had to understand, first of all, that there were no other gods but their God alone. Later they would be ready or should be ready to understand the compound unity of the one God implicated in the facts that the word for God, Elohim, is masculine plural[209] and that the word for one, *echad*, can be a compound unit[210] used in such relationships as the oneness of a husband and wife which is recorded in Genesis 2:21. However, the emphasis of God's instruction in this pre-stage period was in the oneness of God; this was what the Israelites needed to learn at this time in their development.

---

[209]Francis Brown, S. R. Driver, Charles A. Briggs, and William Gesenius, <u>The New Brown-Driver-Briggs-Gesenius Hebrew and English Lexicon</u> (n.p.: Christian Copyrights, Inc., 1979), 43, #430.

[210]Frank E. Gæbelein, <u>The Expositor's Bible Commentary</u>, vol. 3 (Grand Rapids, MI: Zondervan Publishing House, 1992), 65.

Besides the ritual and codified constitution, God provided the new nation with a set of civil laws. These laws were to give instruction to the Israelites regarding how to live properly, orderly, and in a healthy manner in everyday life in their time frame, environment, and culture. Although they could not understand the reasons why they were to follow specified procedures, they would remain healthy and orderly if they did. God did not explain the "whys" and "wherefores" because as infants they were not able to understand them. Nevertheless, He provided them with a structure within which to live.

Again, the Israelites could not fully understand the ritual, the code, or the civil laws, but the concepts would be ingrained in them from infancy upward. The ritual, code and laws were to honor God, themselves, and others, and Israel was to become a distinct people, separated from the practices of other cultures, with the identity as God's people through whom He would work. They were not ready yet, but God was preparing them from their beginning to have identity and meaning and to represent Him.

Israel remained in the infancy through one-year stage for forty years while they wandered in the wilderness. It took them that long to learn to trust God and to develop into a people who could obey God and be able to inherit Canaan, the land promised to Abraham. At first, a little over a year after their birth, when God encouraged the people to enter Canaan land, promising His miraculous power, they refused. Thirty-eight-plus years later, they had learned a few lessons and were ready to obey God and possess the land.

As Israel was about ready to possess the land, God provided words of encouragement to them as a father to a son stating, "The LORD your God, who is going before you, will fight for you, as he did for you in Egypt, before your very eyes, and in the desert. There you saw how the LORD your God carried you, as a father carries his son, all the way you went until you reached this place" (Deuteronomy 1:30-31, NIV).

Stage One

When the Israelites were ready to graduate to the first stage of Intuitive-Projective Faith, usually occurring in early childhood and the play age, God carefully took His people by the hand and performed another miracle, similar to the one He had performed forty years earlier. He supernaturally parted the Jordan River as He had parted the Red (Reed) Sea and His people crossed over on dry ground. God was showing them that He was the same God who had been with them in their infant and one-year stage in the wilderness and who would be with them in their next stage.

This faith stage is interspersed with control and limited freedom, and Israel began to have a sense of being a free people as land was possessed and settled. In the early years of this stage, Israel also was aware of God in the midst of them, enabling them in conquest. It was at this time that they were freely an obedient people. When the sin of Achan was discovered among them and God exercised His control by withholding His enabling power for conquest, the people quickly removed the sin in their camp and again were able to receive God's supernatural work in their midst (Joshua 7 and 8). When nine and one-half of the tribes thought that the other two and one-half tribes had committed sin by erecting an altar on the west side of the Jordan River, they wisely checked into the matter. However, no action was necessary because they discovered the other tribes had merely erected a symbolic altar to represent their connection and oneness with the other nine and one-half tribes (Joshua 22:9-34). They had not intended to misuse it and worship God there, since they knew worship was only to be made at the Tabernacle location. Consequently, there was no wrong doing, but if there had been, the rest of Israel would have removed the wrong from their midst.

In this developmental stage, Israel began to formulate an identity of obedience to God as self-awareness and limited autonomy developed. Also, perception through what was fancifully observed began to occur. Thus, it was at this time that ritualization patterns began to take root and Israel began to notice the patterns of ritual and interaction with God and others.

Throughout the early part of this stage, in the days of their leader Joshua and the elders after him, the Israelites remained obedient to God as they took their place in the land and began to settle down (Joshua 24:31; Judges 2:7). However, after the time frame of Joshua and his elders, the people began to exercise their autonomy and freedom to break away from God. They began to notice the religious practices of the people around them, and these practices appeared attractive to them. This produced a cycle of events from the perspective of the exercise of God's control and the people's freedom.

At their young age, the Israelites were drawn by what they observed. Their neighbors to the west of them lived in the shephelah territory of the valleys and the fertile coastal plains. They appeared to have abundant crops as the result of their "pagan" religious practices which involved fertility rites of temple prostitution as well as other immorality. As the Israelites moved away from God during a time of peace and protection given them by God and as they entered into the practices of their "pagan" neighbors, they fell into apostasy. As a result, God in exercising His control, withdrew His blessings upon them of protection and provision and caused them to be oppressed by neighboring nations. Eventually, they repented for their actions and cried out to God for deliverance. During this young period of their development, God faithfully responded each time to their pleas for help and provided a deliverer or judge who, most often as a military leader, would free them from oppression. Then the period of peace and provision of blessings from God would occur again.

This cycle was repeated over and over and is called the period of the judges in Scripture (see Book of Judges). It involved cycles of events, each of which contained the following five phases:

1. A period of peace and prosperity under God as the Israelites lived obediently;
2. A period of apostasy, a falling away from God and adoption of pagan religious practices;
3. A period of oppression by enemies, usually involving lack of provision and hardship;
4. A period of repentance and crying out to God for help; and
5. A period in which God faithfully sent a deliverer or judge to free the people from oppression and lead them back to obedience under God, which ushered in a time of peace again, repeating the cycle.

Each cycle seemed to go in a downhill spiral, with apostasy becoming worse, oppression worse, and the cry for help less sincere in repentance each time. However, God remained faithful, exercising His control when necessary for correction and chastisement, as a father with a son, and providing relief from oppression upon repentance.

God was attempting to mold His people into His capable representatives, which would provide for their identity and meaning. It would take much time with God gradually giving them more and more freedom with less and less control as they would develop from one stage to the next. And they would exercise their freedom, sometimes wisely and sometimes unwisely. But eventually, through much patience, instruction, and training by God, and many heartaches to themselves, they would become what they were intended to become, God's representatives to the world to draw others to Him.

Stage Two

Stage Two faith is called by Fowler Mythic-Literal Faith. This stage involves the capacity to think concretely and logically from a literal perspective. It is the school-age stage in the developmental process. In this stage the world appears more orderly than it did previously and community myths and morés become important although their perceived meanings are on a literal, surface level.

With respect to the nation of Israel at this stage, they were ready to leave where they were in stage one and to acquire more freedom in their actions. Now they were more aware of the structure of the world around them and desired to be like the other nations in the aspect of government. Up until now, God had been their king in a theocracy-type set up, and now they were rejecting Him as king. In response to their request for a king as in other nations, God warned them what it would be like. However, He gave them their request as a loving parent who is teaching a child. Parents often will try to guide children, but if their instruction and guidance goes unheeded, they sometimes may give children what they desire and allow them to suffer the consequences so that they can learn thereby that the parent knew better all along. The scenario of Israel's desire for a king and God's response is provided in the following Scripture passages from 1 Samuel 8:4-22 (NIV):

All the elders of Israel gathered together and came to Samuel at Ramah. They said to him, "You are old, and your sons do not walk in your ways; now appoint a king to lead us, such as all the other nations have."

But when they said, "Give us a king to lead us," this displeased Samuel; so he prayed to the LORD. And the LORD told him: "Listen to all that the people are saying to you; it is not you they have rejected, but they have rejected me as their king. As they have done from the day I brought them up out of Egypt until this day, forsaking me and serving other gods, so they are doing to you. Now listen to them; but warn them solemnly and let them know what the king who will reign over them will do."

Samuel told all the words of the LORD to the people who were asking him for a king. He said, "This is what the king who will reign over you will do: He will take your sons and make them serve with his chariots and horses, and they will run in front of his chariots. Some he will assign to be commanders of thousands and commanders of fifties, and others to plow his ground and reap his harvest, and still others to make weapons of war and equipment for his chariots. He will take your daughters to be perfumers and cooks and bakers. He will take the best of your fields and vineyards and olive groves and give them to his attendants. He will take a tenth of your grain and of your vintage and give it to his officials and attendants. Your menservants and maidservants and the best of your cattle and donkeys he will take for his own use. He will take a tenth of your flocks, and you yourselves will become his slaves. When that day comes, you will cry out for relief from the king you have chosen, and the LORD will not answer you in that day."

But the people refused to listen to Samuel. "No!" they said. "We want a king over us. Then we will be like all the other nations, with a king to lead us and to go out before us and fight our battles."

When Samuel heard all that the people said, he repeated it before the LORD. The LORD answered, "Listen to them and give them a king."

Thus, God provided His people more autonomy in giving them a king and allowed them to learn from their mistakes. Here, He said He would not interact in their affairs in the same manner He had done previously. If they would cry out to Him because of the consequences of their actions, He would not immediately respond to their pleas for help as He had done in the past. They would have to learn from their mistakes and reap the results. Then they would have to repent for their wrong doing and change their ways, seeking Him with all their heart and showing they were sincere through living an obedient life style as His people.

God had not indicated that He would leave His people, but in giving them more freedom, they needed to reap the results of their actions without immediate intervention on His part. This also was a type of training and instruction of His people, as a father with a growing child.

The first king God gave His people was Saul, a person who had the appearance and stature of a king, being handsome and head and shoulders above everyone else (1 Samuel 9:2; 10:23). However, appearance is not everything, and in Saul's case it was deceiving. He was not strong in character and in actions was disobedient toward God's instructions.

Eventually, Saul was replaced by David, a person who was considered to be an obedient man after God's own heart (Acts 13:22). David honored God before all of His people by placing the Ark of the Covenant, which was symbolic of God's presence, in the midst of the nation of Israel, signifying that God was dwelling in the midst of His people. David even instituted worship and praise before the symbolic presence of God. Although David was king, he honored God above himself. During David's time frame, the people became grounded in proper ritualistic worship and in obedience. The morés of the community were deemed to be important from a literal perspective. As a result, God gave His people increased territory, wealth, and victory over their enemies.

Solomon was David's son whom David appointed to replace him just prior to death. He began as a godly king and remained so for about twenty-five years into his reign. He had the Temple of God built in Jerusalem, replacing the temporary Tabernacle, and looked to God for wisdom in adequately governing God's people. God answered His request for wisdom, and as a result, he was noted as the wisest person on earth (1 Kings 3:9-12; 4:29-31; 5:12). His also was a peaceful and prosperous reign as a blessing from God (1 Kings 3:13; 1 Kings 10). However, eventually Solomon tried to keep up his image in his own power; he married foreign women to form peace alliances with other nations and built these women houses and temples for their own gods right in the land of Israel. As a result, idolatry was introduced officially by the king into God's nation of Israel which pulled many of the people away from worship of the true God.

The actions of kings and leaders are important because these people are very influential over others. When the people see the one in responsible leadership position falling away from God, they follow suit, as a sheep with a shepherd. Thus, the leader leads the community in the establishing of its morés and in their observance. Again, this is the Mythical-Literal Faith stage and the kingly leaders were very influential in the religious practices of Israel. The observance of God's rituals were only on a surface level at this stage. Therefore, as the king would change the religious practices, the people readily would follow because their depth of understanding was limited.

God allowed His people to reap the consequences of their apostasy by dividing the kingdom after Solomon's death. God still had sovereign control, but used it sparingly in the attempt to give Israel the opportunity to learn and grow in decision-making power. However, as a parent will not allow a child to go too far away on its own, God occasionally would intervene in Israel's affairs to guide them in the proper direction. He often used events as well as His prophets to communicate warnings and provide an alternative course of action from the path they were on. The alternative path was designed to provide blessings, encouragement and hope for His people if followed.

During the divided monarchy period in which Israel existed as two nations, the northern kingdom retained the name of Israel while the southern kingdom was known as Judah. God's people grew further and further away from Him at this time in their development. Finally, God intervened dramatically and removed His people from their land. First, He removed Israel because progression away from Him occurred more rapidly there. Next, he removed Judah when they eventually reached the same state of apostasy.

Removal from the land did not mean that God had abandoned His people as a nation or a "son." However, it did mean that they were not acting like His people and that they needed a wake-up call (individually many had forsaken God). Removal of God's people from their land provided advancement into the next stage of faith development.

Stage Three

This is the stage referred to as Synthetic-Conventional Faith. This stage involves many changes, both physical and mental, and is considered the period of adolescence. At first, life is difficult and unfamiliar at this stage because of the changes. People feel awkward and disoriented. But then a sense of normality transpires as one adjusts and finds a sense of belonging and a type of identity and meaning in group association with others of like mind. It is during this period that one begins to develop abstract thinking.

With respect to Israel, this stage involved the period from the exile, through the post exile, into the approximately four hundred silent years when God did not communicate to humanity specifically through His prophets, and on into the beginning of the New Testament period. This period comprised a great deal of change and adjustment to change.

First of all, God's people found themselves displaced and were not sure who they were. Was God still with them, were they still His people? How could they approach Him without benefit of the ritualistic Temple worship? Could they have an identity of their own without their land? Should they settle down or be ready to return to their homeland? These were questions which indicated that the Israelites were becoming capable of the beginning stages of formal operational thought, or in other words, abstract thinking. They were beginning to think beyond what they could observe.

The exile was an awkward time for Israel at first. But God was there for them. He spoke through His prophets Daniel and Ezekiel and had spoken already through Jeremiah and others to prepare them for this time.

It was a great encouragement for God's people to see Daniel, who was one of them, elevated to a prominent position in the Babylonian kingdom and at the same time uphold his worship of God and maintain his ritualistic practice of prayer three times a day in front of a window facing Jerusalem (Daniel 2:48; 6:10). Ezekiel also was used of God to encourage the elders of God's people (Ezekiel 8:1; 14:1; 20:1). In addition, it appears that small religious cell groups, later known as synagogues, were formulated at this time to maintain and establish the identity of God's people and to encourage worship and obedience to Him along with instruction from the Scriptures which had been written by then. It is most likely that Ezekiel was responsible for the establishment of these religious groups.[211]

It is interesting that, although it was not possible to perform the Temple ritual in approaching God, God still responded to the remnant of His people in exile who sought Him. This indicates that the ritual was merely an instructional tool and that God was interested in the meaning it represented.

The small synagogue cell groups served to stabilize God's people in the midst of the radical change of being deported from their homeland and interspersed among people of other cultures and religious beliefs. Instead of assimilating this time, God's people maintained their own identity in exile, at least a remnant of them did. Typical of this stage of development, they attached themselves to the small groups for meaningful identity. The synagogues served this purpose as the Israelites were reminded there of their identity as God's people even in the midst of exile. Also typical was the influence of respected leaders of their group. Daniel and Ezekiel served this function, being part of the larger group of Israel within which the smaller groups were based.

As identity was stabilized and as a remnant became established that honored and obeyed God, God provided for their return to their homeland. This also involved adjustment since the land had been destroyed by their Babylonian captives about seventy years earlier, but they had the benefit of group identity to carry them along. It took a while to establish homes and fertile crops and to rebuild their Temple

---

[211]J. D. Douglas, org. ed., <u>New Bible Dictionary</u>, 2nd ed. (Wheaton: Tyndale House Publishers, Inc., 1982), s.v. "Synagogue," by C. L. Feinberg.

so they could reinstitute the proper ritual for religious worship of God.

In the process of rebuilding the foundation of the Temple, their strong group ties became evident when they would not allow the northern Samaritans[212] to help them in the building (Ezra 4:2-3). Almost a hundred years later, a similar situation occurred as Nehemiah led God's people in the rebuilding of Jerusalem and its walls. At that time, when the Samaritans ridiculed the project, Nehemiah indicated that they had "no heritage or right or memorial in Jerusalem" (Nehemiah 2:20, NKJV). The identity of God's people was not to be contaminated with others who would pull them away from God.

However, Israel was not without its internal problems. In fact, as the people settled in their homeland after the exile, during the post exile time frame, some did begin to intermarry with the women of the land and their children were raised far from God. This fact became of great concern to God's leaders, Ezra, Nehemiah and Malachi. If left unchecked, God's people would again lose their distinct identity and possibly again would be removed from their land. The situation was serious, so serious that the leaders under Ezra, along with the people, decided that it would be best if those who had married heathen women would divorce them or put them away if they would not convert to the Israelite faith. Those who chose not to respond in this manner would be removed from the group of the people of God and would lose their identity as such (Ezra 9 and 10). The situation was the reverse in Malachi's time frame. Then some of God's people divorced their Israelite wives and married heathen women (Malachi 2:14-16). This also would cause loss of identity as the children from the new unions would be raised without knowledge of God. God used Malachi to confront that

---

[212]The Samaritans were a mixture of the poor Israelites left in the northern territory of Israel at the time of the Assyrian conquest and exile and of other conquered peoples who were imported into that territory. Their religious practices became a syncretic mixture.

problem along with others which had gradually crept into the practices of the Israelites.

Apparently God's words through the prophet Malachi had an impact upon the people of God. Thereafter, according to history, they maintained their identity and remained separated from the heathen practices of others. Even when the Grecians became the dominant rulers of their part of the world and amalgamated various cultures and religious practices, the Israelites would not acquiesce, but retained their own identity as God's people. This was progress from their former ways. This adolescent, Synthetic-Conventional type of faith period helped in the firm establishment of their identity as God's people. Thus, they did not lose their identity as many other cultures did under the Grecian assimilation influence. They remained a distinct people ready for the birth of their Messiah (the anointed one) who would lead them into further truth and purpose as God's people. Now they were ready for the next faith stage of development.

<u>Stage Four</u>

Individuative-Reflective Faith is the name of stage four. It pertains to the period of young adulthood. It is at this time that the ability for critical and reflective thinking becomes prominent in a more advanced method of abstract thinking than was present in the previous stage. Now identity with a group does not have the hold it once did. Reasons for group identification and its basis for morés are considered. One now assumes personal responsibility for beliefs and associations and actions. In the process, one analyzes symbols or rituals which were used in the past as a matter of form. Now the symbols are demythologized and their meaning is extracted. New commitments are considered as one gains a new, orderly perspective of self and the world, of identity, meaning, and values.

Israel came into this stage with a firmly established identity. It can be seen in the attitudes of the scribes and Pharisees as recorded in the gospels. There was a rigidity evident in their attitude; they considered that their ways and ideas were the only ones which were correct and right before God. This attitude can occur as one remains in a stage three faith perspective and thinks narrowly and idealistically that one's own group is perfect and the only group to be considered. People with this attitude become very judgmental of others who do not share their viewpoints. This was evident with the scribes and Pharisees of Jesus' day who believed because they were descendants of Abraham and followed certain rituals that they were secure in their relationship with God (Matthew 3:7). In fact, they went so far as to condemn Jesus for associating with outsiders, those not of their religious group, who did not adhere to their elaborate and specific laws and rituals and procedures (Matthew 9:11; 15:1-2; Mark 2:16; 7:1-5; Luke 5:30; 15:2). Eventually the scribes and Pharisees sought to destroy Jesus because he did not follow their legalistic procedures and because he was advocating beliefs which were unsettling to those of their group (Matthew 12:14; Luke 6:7; 11:53). However, Jesus accused these scribes and Pharisees of being hypocritical, formally going through ritualistic observances but being far from the symbolic meaning in their hearts (Matthew 23:1-33; Mark 7:5-6; Luke 11:44).

An example of the stage three faith at this time was provided when Jesus commented that his followers and disciples were to eat his flesh and drink his blood. This was offensive to the literal, concrete, conventional thinkers of stage three faith who had not yet developed their beginning formal operational and abstract thinking capacities, especially because drinking blood was forbidden to God's people (Genesis 9:4). However, Jesus was speaking in a metaphorical and spiritual sense since he was the giver and provider of true life (John 6:47-58, 63).

The scribes and Pharisees were typical of an extreme stage three faith. They were not able to see past their rituals into their meanings. Therefore, they condemned everyone who was not of their own special group, a group which they considered to be privileged with God.

However, other Israelites were beginning to break out of stage three faith and into the more developed and critical thinking of stage four faith. It was hard to break away from their previous identity with the "in group" of God's people so to speak. But Jesus offered them deeper insights into the foundation of their previous identity. He provided reasons and meanings for their ritualistic procedures which went deeper than merely outward observance. In stage four faith some were ready for their symbols and rituals to be demythologized and for meaning to come to the forefront of their perspective. Jesus encouraged these responsive individuals to assume personal responsibility for their lives and provided them with a depth of meaning that they had not known previously. He opened up their eyes to what it really meant to be God's people. Yes, it involved a paradigm shift which was difficult. But it also provided these people with a sense of life and freedom from the bondage of the oppressive burden of the law as interpreted by the scribes and Pharisees.

These people came to realize that the law was merely a shadow, a representation, an illustration, a symbol or a figure of what was to come (Hebrews 9:8-18; 10:1-14). Christ Jesus was the fulfillment of the previous type which served as a "schoolmaster," "tutor," "disciplinarian" until he came (Galatians 3:24-25; Hebrews 7:18-19). Now they were no longer subject to a "schoolmaster" as if they were little children who did not know the basics. Now they were of age and able to apply the truth of the previous type to their lives. Now they were able to comprehend that Christ Jesus was their provision for life, something which the old law could not do (Galatians 3:21) but which pointed to him as the one who should come through the symbolic examples of Tabernacle worship.

These stage four Israelites came to believe that Jesus offered life through himself as the Son of God, who was the fulfillment of the Old Testament ritual. They believed that He was the Lamb of God who was the real sacrifice on the altar to atone for humanity's sin.[213] They realized that the Old Testament lamb whose blood was shed on the brazen altar was only symbolic of what the true Lamb of God was to accomplish through his death, which was the provision of cleansing from sin in order to approach and be restored to fellowship with God. They realized the effectiveness of this provision as they applied the true Lamb's cleansing blood to their lives.

Because sin or transgression or rebellion from God resulted in physical and spiritual death, humanity needed cleansing or the atonement of sin to gain fellowship with the holy God, both in this life and eternally. In other words, sin caused humanity to be separated from the life-giving presence of God. As a result, death occurred immediately from a spiritual perspective when Adam and Eve rebelled, and it occurred gradually from a physical perspective. All who have been born since Adam and Eve have inherited a nature to rebel from God, and all do rebel. However, as Adam and Eve were given the choice to obey God or to be lord of self, all humanity since Adam and Eve have been given the same choice. If they choose self, they continue on as they are. If they choose God as Lord of their lives, they have His provision of cleansing from wrong doing provided by the blood of the true Lamb of God, as represented by animal sacrifice in the Old Testament ritual but as carried out through Jesus' death on the cross.

The problem for the Israelites in this scenario was that Jesus claimed not only to be the Son of God but God Himself, one of the persons of the Godhead. To the Jews this idea appeared as blasphemy. One claiming to be God while repre-senting the God in heaven appeared to contradict the scriptural statement recorded in Deuteronomy 6:4 that there was only one true God, a statement that they finally had come to believe as truth. It appeared to them that Jesus was claiming that there were two gods, which was a contradiction of Scripture and truth as they perceived it.

---

[213]See Isaiah 53:7-8; John 1:29; Acts 8:32-35; 1 Corinthians 5:7; 1 Peter 1:18-19.

Theologically, however, Jesus had to be God in order to atone for sins because a sinless sacrifice was necessary. Yet all humanity had sinned since Adam and Eve. Humanity was in a predicament. There was a need for an adequate sacrifice, but humanity could not provide one. God, the Father, solved the problem by sending His Son, the second person of the Trinity in human form. Actually, the Son added a human nature to his divine nature without destroying the integrity of either nature, and he became the God-man. How this was possible is beyond human comprehension. Yet the Son, Christ Jesus, remained the same divine person as he had been from all eternity past but with a human nature added. As the God-man, Christ Jesus could be tempted or exposed to sin without sinning, because his holy divine nature was not compatible with sin. As the God-man, Christ Jesus remained sinless.[214] And as the God-man, Christ Jesus could die as a vicarious and efficacious, sinless sacrifice to atone for humanity's sin. As God, Christ would not have been able to die because God is life, but as the God-man this somehow and inexplicably became possible. If Christ had been merely human, he would not have been sinless and could not have atoned for sin. The incarnation of Christ is a paradox which cannot be explained. Yet theologically, he must be the God-man as Scripture verifies,[215] or there is no hope for sinful humanity to be restored to fellowship with the holy God.

The fact that it was predicted that Christ would be resurrected from death, never to be subject to death again,[216] and that he stated he would rise from the dead in three days,[217] and that he did rise as he said he would[218] is verification of who he claimed to be and what he claimed to accomplish. He was God incarnate in human flesh, the God-man, who

---

[214]See 2 Corinthians 5:21; Hebrews 4:15; 7:26; 1 Peter 2:22; 1 John 3:5.

[215]See Isaiah 7:14; 9:6-7; Micah 5:2; John 1:1-2, 14; Philippians 2:6-8; 1 Timothy 3:16; Hebrews 1:8; 2:14.

[216]See Job 19:25; Psalm 16:9-10; Isaiah 53:10-11.

[217]See Matthew 12:40; 27:63; Mark 8:31; 9:31; 10:33-34; John 2:19-22.

[218]See Acts 1:3; 2:24, 31, 32; 4:10; 17:31; Romans 1:4; 4:25; 8:34; 1 Corinthians 15:4-8, 12-23; 1 Peter 1:21.

effectively and adequately atoned for the sins of the world. The only responsibility on the individual's part was to receive the cleansing which Christ, the God-man offered in order for the atonement to be applied personally. It was to be a free gift available to all who would receive it.

By this fourth faith stage of development, the Israelites were supposed to be able to make the transition from the idea of one God to the idea of one God as a compound unity in the form of the Trinity, God the Father, God the Son, and God the Holy Spirit. The idea was before them all along in the particular wording of Deuteronomy 6:4,[219] and now was the time for this insight to come to light. It was a difficult concept for those who could only see the one paradigm. When they were supposed to worship only one God, they apostatized to other gods. Now when they were to receive the concept that their one God is a compound unity, they finally were firmly established in the fact that there was only one God and could not comprehend the developed concept of compound unity. However, some of God's people did receive the new concept. They applied to themselves personally the atoning sacrifice of the resurrected Christ because their belief and faith was founded upon the fact of Christ's resurrection (1 Corinthians 15:12-23).

Another concept which was difficult for the Israelites was that the atonement provided by Jesus was available to all who would receive it.[220] They had been used to the idea that they were a favored people, God's people no less, and now He was opening up the doors to all who would come. In their exclusive attitude, the Israelites had lost sight of their meaning as God's people; they were to draw others to Him so that whosoever wanted to do so could come. They were supposed to be an inclusive people, drawing others to God; however, they had become introverted and of no spiritual value to themselves or others. They still had identity but it was no

---

[219]See other Old Testament Scriptures such as Isaiah 7:6 and Daniel 7:9-14.

[220]See John 3:14-18; 2 Corinthians 5:15-19; Galatians 3:26-29; 1 Timothy 2:4-6; 2 Peter 3:9.

longer meaningful. They had lost their purpose and significance.

But those Israelites who had made the transition to stage four faith found their true identity as God's people. They began to realize their true purpose and meaning as it was revealed and renewed at this stage. God provided these people the following words of encouragement from 1 Peter 1:18-2:10 (NKJV) which contain the repetition of the original, but conditional, purpose set forth for Israel from Exodus 19:4-6 (highlighted):

You were not redeemed with corruptible things, [like] silver or gold, from your aimless conduct [received] by tradition from your fathers, but with the precious blood of Christ, as of a lamb without blemish and without spot. He indeed was foreordained before the foundation of the world, but was manifest in these last times for you who through Him believe in God, who raised Him from the dead and gave Him glory, so that your faith and hope are in God.

Since you have purified your souls in obeying the truth through the Spirit in sincere love of the brethren, love one another fervently with a pure heart, having been born again, not of corruptible seed but incorruptible, through the word of God which lives and abides forever, because "All flesh [is] as grass, And all the glory of man as the flower of the grass. The grass withers, and its flower falls away, but the word of the LORD endures forever." Now this is the word which by the gospel was preached to you.

Therefore, laying aside all malice, all deceit, hypocrisy, envy, and all evil speaking, as newborn babes, desire the pure milk of the word, that you may grow thereby, if indeed you have tasted that the Lord [is] gracious.

Coming to Him [as to] a living stone, rejected indeed by men, but chosen by God [and] precious, you also, as living stones, are being built up a spiritual house, a holy priesthood, to offer up spiritual sacrifices acceptable to God through Jesus Christ. Therefore it is also contained in the Scripture, "Behold, I lay in Zion A chief cornerstone, elect, precious, and he who believes on Him will by no means be put to shame." Therefore, to you who believe, [He is] precious; but to those who are disobedient, "The stone which the builders rejected has become the chief cornerstone," and "A stone of stumbling and a rock of offense." They stumble, being disobedient to the word, to which they also were appointed. But **you [are] a chosen generation, a royal priesthood, a holy nation, His own special people**, that you may proclaim the praises of Him who called you out of darkness into His marvelous light.

These Israelites of stage four faith broke away from the security of belonging to the group made up of Synthetic-Conventional faith-type Israelites. They reflected upon the symbols and ritual which had been so important to them and extracted their true meanings. They realized that Christ Jesus was the fulfillment of their heritage and that they would be true Israelites and fulfilled according to their purpose in him. They now assumed responsibility for their actions, personally committing to the one they believed to be the hoped-for Messiah-Prophet-Redeemer-King prophesied and prefigured throughout the Old Testament.[221] As a result of their belief, they had come of age as full-grown sons as the Apostle Paul indicates in Galatians 4:1-7 (NIV):

What I am saying is that as long as the heir is a child, he is no different from a slave, although he owns the whole estate. He is subject to guardians and trustees until the time set by his father. So also, when we were children, we were in slavery under the basic principles

---

[221] See Genesis 3:15; Deuteronomy 18:18; 2 Samuel 7:12-16; Job 19:25; Isaiah 7:14; 9:6-7; Zechariah 6:12-13; Malachi 3:1; Hebrews 9:9-10.

of the world. But when the time had fully come, God sent his Son, born of a woman, born under law, to redeem those under law, that we might receive the full rights of sons. Because you are sons, God sent the Spirit of his Son into our hearts, the Spirit who calls out, ["Abba], {Aramaic for [Father]} Father." So you are no longer a slave, but a son; and since you are a son, God has made you also an heir.

These stage four Israelites did not abandon their heritage and their people. They entered into the realization of what it meant to be true Israelites. However, the stage three Israelites began to persecute them. Thus, they could not worship in the Israelite synagogues. These people banded together and began meeting in homes to worship God through their newly found perspective and Redeemer, Christ Jesus. Eventually, these people became known as Christians (Acts 11:26) because of their association with the risen Christ. And eventually they also became known as the body of believers who made up the Church (Acts 2:47). The Church was not a new entity; it was the outgrowth of the foundation of Israel (Ephesians 2:20). In essence it was the label for the "young adults" of this faith stage and the "adults" of the later stages who were considered the "bride of Christ."[222] These "young adults" had found someone in whom to place their loyalty, someone in whom to commit themselves and their lives. Typical of this stage, the young adult-type person of Israelite faith now was able to risk destroying the individuality of this stage by fusing it with another, which was achieved through intimacy.[223] This provided God's people with a renewed

---

[222]See Ephesians 5:22-32; Revelation 19:7-9; 21:9. Israel in the Old Testament had been considered the wife of God (see the book of Hosea; Isaiah 50:1; 54:6; Jeremiah 3:8, 14).

[223]This idea is in the context of Erikson's sixth stage of psychosocial development, but it also seems applicable here. Léonie Sugarman, Life-Span Development: Concepts, Theories and Interventions (New York: Methuen & Company, Limited, 1986), 89.

identity and meaning. They were Christians, representatives of Christ Jesus.

Stage Five

Stage five faith is considered to occur in adulthood, if at all. It is represented by the name of Conjunctive Faith and is the first of two mature faith stages. It involves a more balanced view of self and the world than stage four faith which is more apt to pull away from group association if its meanings are no longer deemed to be important from a reflective, critical thinking viewpoint. This stage takes a new look at symbols combined with their meanings, and it also allows meaningful values from the past to be incorporated in the present. Altruism also is characteristic of this faith stage, with the desire to enhance the lives of others by sharing what one has learned to be meaningful.

With respect to God's people at this stage, they were not so quick to cast off the symbols of their heritage but to combine them with their meanings for deeper understanding. Although they would no longer practice the ancient rituals because they were fulfilled in Christ Jesus, they valued them for the insights they could provide. Thus, the past became meaningful to these people at this stage. It was viewed as an instructor to perceive the depths and foundation of the present. But at this stage, their past did not limit them; it provided a meaningful structure for their current perspective of faith. They saw the past in a new light because of where they were in the present.

However, God's people did not cast off the practice of rituals altogether. The Passover observance was to be re-enacted with the ritual of what became known as the Lord's Supper or Communion. This ritualistic event was to be observed regularly by the Christians to remind them of their provision in Christ, the ultimate Passover Lamb, and of their future with him eternally (Luke 22:14-20; 1 Corinthians 11:23-26). Also, they were to observe the ritual of water baptism upon confession of faith in Christ Jesus. This was to be observed once at the beginning of their Christian life and represented death to sinful self and rising anew to life in Christ, both in this life and for eternity (Matthew 28:19; Romans 6:3-5). Thus, it was seen that ritual was helpful as long as its meaning was tied to the symbolism. And the above two rituals served as a reminder and teacher of what was important to the Christian.

Also, at this stage, God's people, the Church, began to look outward. They were excited about their identity as God's people, and it was difficult to keep their excitement to themselves. Now they wanted to share the benefits they had received with others. They wanted to represent God and draw others to Him. They were ready to take their proper place in the world through the enabling power provided by Christ Jesus. They were ready to be his witnesses, which was their true purpose all along. But it took this stage to realize it. Now they wanted to fulfill the renewed or Great Commission, representing Him to others as Christ had commanded them to do (Matthew 28:18-20, NRSV):

> Jesus came and said to them, "All authority in heaven and on earth has been given to me. Go therefore and make disciples of all nations, baptizing them in the name of the Father and of the Son and of the Holy Spirit, and teaching them to obey everything that I have commanded you. And remember, I am with you always, to the end of the age."

Thus, this period was a fruitful time for God's people. And it was intended to be so. It was an alive stage and a helpful stage. Consequently, it was a meaningful stage both for God's people and others. It was a time in which a reinterpreted Golden Rule was applied, "Do to another what will advance the other's growth even as it advances your own."[224] And as God's people began to fulfill their purpose, the Church grew rapidly (Acts 2:41; 4:4: 6:7), and many others were brought into fellowship with God.

---

[224]Erik Erikson, *The Life Cycle Completed*, 93.

Characteristics of Maslow's self-actualization stage, which is at the pinnacle of his hierarchy of needs chart, are seen in this fifth faith stage. According to Maslow's definition for self-actualization, it is an "ongoing actualization of potentials, capacities and talents, as fulfillment of mission (or call, fate, destiny, or vocation)." People at this stage are "altruistic, dedicated, self-transcending, and social,"[225] according to Maslow. Erickson's psychosocial stage of Generativity also corresponds to this outward stage of concern for others.

Thus, it is evident that this fifth stage of faith development is a mature stage and corresponds to other mature stages of human development. It was so for God's people who were now known as Christians and belonged to the Church. They willingly shared of themselves and their faith for the betterment of others. They became God's witnesses to the world.

Stage Six

The last faith stage is stage six, Universalizing Faith. It is the second and last of the two mature stages of faith. This is not a populous stage; very few reach it. But those who do are totally sold out and totally committed to what they believe. They do not compromise their beliefs, but maintain the integrity for which they stand. They view their beliefs as universal and applicable to the world. Therefore, these people at this stage also want to share what they perceive as valuable for others as in the stage five faith. However, now their desire is to transform society according to the universal truth as they see it.

This last stage faith also was apparent in God's people, the Church, as recorded in Scripture. However, it was not seen in the total Church at that time, but in some churches and in some individuals who made up the total Church. The same was true of Israel of old. Some within developed to their appropriate faith stage and some did not.

With respect to individuals who were leaders in the Church, Stephen, Paul, and John are examples of mature stage

---

[225] Abraham H. Maslow, <u>Toward a Psychology of Being</u>, 2nd ed., 25, vi.

six faith. Although Stephen did not live long, Paul had opportunity to encourage the churches to follow his own dedicated example (Philippians 3:17; 2 Thessalonians 3:9). And John was a pillar who was an encouragement to many.

These people can be considered radicals for their sold-out dedication in serving the Lord. And their transforming message, which they believed to be of universal application, may have been revolutionary for their time and environment. However, they did not attempt to overthrow principalities and powers of this world. They were not revolutionaries in that sense. But they were totally committed and would not compromise their beliefs and testimonies even if it meant death. For Stephen it did mean death; he became the first Christian martyr (Acts 6:87:60). And for Paul it meant much persecution, imprisonment, and possibly even death at one point, but if so he was revived.[226] Regarding death and his dedication, he stated in Philippians 1:20-24 (NRSV):

> It is my eager expectation and hope that I will not be put to shame in any way, but that by my speaking with all boldness, Christ will be exalted now as always in my body, whether by life or by death. For to me, living is Christ and dying is gain. If I am to live in the flesh, that means fruitful labor for me; and I do not know which I prefer. I am hard pressed between the two: my desire is to depart and be with Christ, for that is far better; but to remain in the flesh is more necessary for you.

Here was a man who knew what he believed; there were no doubts. He was sold out, and he wanted his life to be totally given over for the transformation of others in the Christian faith. However, personally, he preferred to depart this life and to be in the presence of Christ. When he approached death, possibly at the hands of the Roman emperor Nero, he had no regrets with how his Christian life had been

---

[226]Compare Acts 14:19-20 with 2 Corinthians 12:1-6.

spent, and he looked forward to his glorious, eternal future. His comment is recorded in 2 Timothy 4:6-8 (NIV):

> For I am already being poured out like a drink offering, and the time has come for my departure. I have fought the good fight, I have finished the race, I have kept the faith. Now there is in store for me the crown of righteousness, which the Lord, the righteous Judge, will award to me on that day—and not only to me, but also to all who have longed for his appearing.

The Apostle John was banished as a lowest criminal to the Isle of Patmos in the later years of his life by the Romans for the testimony of his faith. Yet he did not compromise. It was there that God gave him the revelation of Jesus Christ which he recorded in the book of Revelation. Even in old age and banished from society, his life was meaningful and helpful. He remained sold out to the end, a good example of the sixth and last stage of mature faith development.

As recorded in Scripture, there are evidences of churches which were a type of the sixth stage of faith. One church consisted of the Thessalonians of whom it is recorded 1 Thessalonians 1:6-10 (NRSV):

> You became imitators of us and of the Lord, for in spite of persecution you received the word with joy inspired by the Holy Spirit, so that you became an example to all the believers in Macedonia and in Achaia. For the word of the Lord has sounded forth from you not only in Macedonia and Achaia, but in every place your faith in God has become known, so that we have no need to speak about it. For the people of those regions report about us what kind of welcome we had among you, and how you turned to God from idols, to serve a living and true God, and to wait for his Son from heaven, whom he raised from the dead— Jesus, who rescues us from the wrath that is coming.

Here, it is seen that the Thessalonians even received the word in the midst of persecution and that they did so joyfully. Persecution was not going to deter them from receiving the benefits of the gospel, nor from sharing it boldly. Later, when Paul wrote to them in 2 Thessalonians, he commended them for their steadfastness in persecutions and trials and afflictions and for their loving attitude toward one another (2 Thessalonians 1:3-4). They were not self-centered. They were strong in their faith, and they remained a good example of what the living Church should be like, a true, mature stage six faith church.

The church of Smyrna appears to be another stage six church. Revelation 2:8-11 records that this church suffered and would continue to suffer tribulation. However, in their affliction and although they were poor, it is stated that they had works. Since no chastisement or condemnation was given to them, it seems apparent that their works were godly works on behalf of others. Thus, they probably were a mature church which had an outward perspective of helping others in spite of their own difficult predicament. Also, they were given encouragement to be faithful even unto death, which seems to indicate that they would have to die for their faith. Apparently they were willing to do so. They appear to be totally committed and were encouraged in what they would have to face.

Another mature church according to Revelation 3:7-13 was the Philadelphia church. They also had works, as the Smyrna church, which were not condemned. Therefore, they probably were godly works which were in consideration of others. The text indicates that they had little strength or were not strong. This mostly likely refers to numbers. They presumably were a small church. And yet they were able to remain faithful, keeping the word of God and not denying Christ's name. They were commended for being patient. The idea is that they were patient in persecutions. Thus, it appears that they had the qualities of mature, stage six faith, being faithful, uncompromising, outward in helping others, and totally committed in the face of persecutions. Therefore, as the Smyrna church, they too received words of encouragement.

Stage six churches were examples of how the mature church ought to be. They were fulfilling their purpose as God had set forth for ancient Israel and as He had renewed for His people who now had developed from Israel into the Church in maturity of faith. An apropos section of Scripture (Colossians 1:25-29, NRSV) by the Apostle Paul sums up the attitude of this mature faith which was his:

> I became its [the church's] servant according to God's commission that was given to me for you, to make the word of God fully known, the mystery that has been hidden throughout the ages and generations but has now been revealed to his saints. To them God chose to make known how great among the Gentiles are the riches of the glory of this mystery, which is Christ in you, the hope of glory. It is he whom we proclaim, warning everyone and teaching everyone in all wisdom, so that we may present everyone mature in Christ. For this I toil and struggle with all the energy that he powerfully inspires within me.

The idea of servanthood is contained therein, portraying service to others. Along the same idea is the fact that Christ was taught and proclaimed so that others could come to maturity of faith also. This was perceived to be universal truth which should transform the world. In order to proclaim this message, Paul was willing to give his total self. All the energy that he had, which was given to him powerfully by the Lord, was committed to this important work. He was solely dedicated to his purpose as a Christian, no matter what, to make the Lord and his truth fully known. Paul had found truth upon which to base his life. This perspective certainly provides identity, meaning and significance to one's life, and one, thus, becomes fulfilled.

Analysis

It has been communicated that God cared for His people as a father does a child. In fact, Scripture provides the metaphor that the nation of Israel was considered God's firstborn son. And according to the faith stages which have been presented, God cared for His son, Israel, along the appropriate parameters of each stage, not expecting more from them past the level of faith they had the capacity to portray. He treated them suitably according to their faith capacity. Thus, He was very patient with them as a father with a child. And He gradually instructed them, laying down foundational principles and building upon them as they were able to receive them. When they became fully grown, He no longer treated them as children, but expected them to come into their own as an adult son, representing Him to others. However, this only could be accomplished through the recognition that Christ Jesus was the fulfillment of the Old Testament foundation, that he was the embodiment of the symbolic ritual of old. As such, they had to recognize him as their Messiah-Redeemer, the true Lamb of God who takes away the sins of the world. Those who responded to this fuller truth in Christ became known as the Church. The Church was not a new entity but an outgrowth from the childhood of Israel into the fully grown, adult son, ready to be God's witnesses to the world.

Maturity was seen as the willingness and desire to share God's message of redemption through Christ to the world. The last meaning-making stage of faith portrayed the ultimate capacity of faith and maturity which was indicated in total commitment without compromise in order to communicate the universal truth of the transforming message of the gospel to the world. Not all New Testament churches reached this last stage, but a few did and they served as examples for the others. And they portrayed fulfillment of God's purpose for His people. They were considered to be His fully grown, mature, adult son with whom He had been so patient. His overall purpose through them finally was beginning to be accomplished. God's efforts had not failed; they just took time. He was a Father who knew how to care for His son through each stage of development. He was wise in all His actions.

PURPOSE

XIV

Identity

The Israelites were always God's people from birth as a "son" or nation, but they did not always act like God's people, especially in their growing up years. The people around them could not always tell that they were different from any other nation or peoples. They did not always show a distinct identity as God's people. Nonetheless, as they developed into their adolescent years, they began to formulate a distinct personality singularly their own. Yes, they became a separated people, especially in the four hundred so-called silent years when God did not speak through His prophets and then on into the beginning of the New Testament time frame; however, they had not yet begun to fulfill their purpose of witnessing to the world. During this latter period of their adolescent years, they became an exclusive people rather than an inclusive people who were to draw others to God.

Characteristic to their identity at this stage of adolescence was strict adherence to laws of rituals, traditions, and extreme cleanliness. Overall, they had become a proud, hypocritical people who considered themselves to be better than others and God's special people. They were self-centered and had not yet realized their purpose for being God's special people. At least these characteristics were true of the scribes and Pharisees who seemed to represent the Israelites.

But their identity as God had intended it to be did not develop until His people began to enter young adulthood so-to-speak. It was here that they began to open their eyes to purpose and meaning. It was here that they saw their identity in a new light through Christ Jesus who was the fulfillment of their symbolic ritual and who was the hope of their redemption. Their background now began to be clear as preparatory for this time in history or this time in their lives. It now was seen to be foundational, instructional and profitable for the understanding of the fulfillment of truth through Christ Jesus.

Through Jesus, they began to understand their purpose for being God's people. They were to be His representatives to the world. However, this was not possible until they received the cleansing and redemption that only He could provide. Their historic rituals were merely types and symbols of the true reality and redemption which was to come. And it came through Jesus Christ the God-man. It was not possible through any other means. Now God's people became redeemed Christians, the people of Christ, the people who would take God's message to the world. Now they had identity which was distinctive, yet meaningful. As they shared their message which gave them identity; it in turn, was beneficial and transforming to others.

Maslow notes that "The loss of illusions and the discovery of identity, though painful at first, can be ultimately exhilarating and strengthening."[227] This became true of the early Christians. As they discarded the misunderstood ideas of their heritage and began to realize the fullness of their intended identity and purpose, they were exhilarated and energized. Thus, it was said of them that they "turned the world upside down" (Acts 17:6, KJV).

Identity has a social aspect. Breger notes that it "is a way of expanding the concept of self to include social factors."[228] It pertains to how one is known in society.

---

[227] Abraham H. Maslow, <u>Toward a Psychology of Being</u>, 2nd ed., 16.

[228] Louis Breger, <u>From Instinct to Identity: The Development of Personality</u>, 329.

Previously the identity of God's people was an isolated identity with respect to others. However, in adulthood through the identity of the Church, it involved interaction with others for their welfare.

Breger also notes that identity "is a complex abstraction" which involves the dimensions of one's past, present, and future.[229] As the past is considered to be in one's present or to influence one's present, so also one's perspective of the future influences one's present. Maslow noted that Freud recognized the connection of the past with the present but adds that the present involves hopes and plans which one prepares for the future in the present. These are seen "in the person in the form of ideals, hopes, duties, tasks, plans, goals, unrealized potentials, mission, fate, destiny, etc." Maslow further comments that for those people who have no hope for the future, life appears to be meaningless. Thus, "one for whom no future exists is reduced to the concrete, to hopelessness, to emptiness."[230]

Concerning God's people, in the maturity of their adult years with respect to stage development, their identity was enhanced with their background of foundational development from their past as God's people and with the perspective of their future which provided them hope (1 Peter 1:3). In fact, their future hope was critical to their identity and beliefs and message they had to share. Because of Jesus' resurrection from the dead, they too had hope that one day they would be resurrected bodily from the dead.[231] But even before that event would occur, upon death they had the hope of spiritually being in the presence of their Lord Christ Jesus (2 Corinthians 5:8; Philippians 1:23). This was based upon their concept of redemption, of being cleansed from their sins by the blood of Jesus and, thus, being able to enter the holy presence of God

---

[229]Ibid., 330.

[230]Abraham H. Maslow, Toward a Psychology of Being, 214.

[231]See Daniel 12:2-3; Romans 6:5; 1 Corinthians 15; 1 Thessalonians 4:13-18; Revelation 20:6.

eternally.[232] This was no idle dream but was promised them by the Lord himself (2 Corinthians 5:8; Philippians 1:23). They believed his words were true because he rose from the dead as he had said he would do, nevermore subject to death. Thus, their future hope became a tremendous motivating factor in their present lives. As God's offspring, it gave them a reason to live and move and have their being (Acts 17:28) because their lives would not end in this temporal realm but would continue on for eternity. Thus, they were significant and what they did in encouragement to others along the same line as theirs was significant for eternity. However, their hope was not just in the life to come but in newness of life in the present which would not cease at the end of this physical life.[233]

Therefore, God's people of the Church had an identity based upon their past as Israelites and upon the present which gave them hope for their future. As part of their identity, they felt compelled to share the fullness of their identity with others. The truth as they had come to realize it was too good to keep to themselves; it was good news (the gospel) which was transforming, and it had transformed them into the purpose God had intended for them as His representatives and witnesses.

Maturity

Maturity brought identity to God's people as it was intended to be. This is because intrinsic to maturity is a balanced view of life with an outward perspective of helping others. God's people were to be God's witnesses; thus, in maturity they fulfilled their purpose by reaching out and sharing their good news with others.

It takes time to establish a firm and distinct identity which does not vacillate, and it takes time to come to maturity. Some never achieve either.   But life becomes more

---

[232]See Leviticus 17:11; Romans 6:23; 2 Corinthians 5:21; Hebrews 9:22, 28.

[233]See John 6:63; 10:10; Romans 6:3-11; 8:2, 10-11; Revelation 22:17.

meaningful and significant when one knows who one is and what one stands for with respect to society and then when one desires to share what has been discovered with others for their benefit also.

Maturity is considered to be the state of being wherein one has reached a balanced view of self and others, with actions reflecting concern for and interest in what is best for the welfare of others as well as society as a whole, without neglecting care of self. God's people, in their adulthood stage of faith, reached this state of maturity in stages five and six. By then, they were known as the Church and they were growing rapidly in numbers because of their mature outlook of sharing. In fact, it was almost impossible for them to do otherwise because of where they were in maturity and because of what they had come to believe. They knew that they had transforming knowledge which the rest of humanity needed for their well-being both in this life and in eternity. They were almost compelled to share this good news.

Along with maturity comes a wise outlook on life, and this is enhanced by the wisdom which is available from God. In fact, He tells His people to ask Him for it (James 1:5). The noted wisdom which Joseph and Daniel of old had even as young men was attributed by them as being from God.[234] And Solomon also had recognized wisdom from God at a young age; in fact, he was wise in the first place to ask for it (1 Kings 3:5-12, 28; 4:29). Although it usually is not evident until maturity of age, Joseph, Daniel, and Solomon had maturity of mind even as young men. But God's people began to receive wisdom in their adult years of stage faith as they matured in faith. At this time, they began to grow in the knowledge of God as revealed through Christ Jesus and the Scripture; this provided them with a mature and wise perspective of God and life. Scripture indicates that the fear of God is the beginning of wisdom as well as knowledge (Psalm 111:10; Proverbs 1:7; 9:10). One must have an awesome respect (fear) for God in order to understand and know Him and gain wisdom

---

[234]See Genesis 41:16, 33-39; Daniel 1:17; 2:27-30, 47-48.

(Proverbs 2:3-7). It is a scriptural fact that lack of knowledge of God is dangerous for one's well-being as indicated in Hosea. Because God's people lacked knowledge of Him in Hosea's day, He said they would perish, and He soon removed them from their land.[235] In the time of the Church, it was the prayer of the Apostle Paul that God's people would grow in the knowledge of Him. Paul kept praying and asking that the God of their Lord Jesus Christ, the glorious Father, may give His people the Spirit of wisdom and revelation, so that they may know Him better.[236]

If people focus on themselves, that is all they can see. But if they focus on God, they also will begin to grow in knowledge and understanding and true wisdom. Figure 7[237] depicts the results of focus, either on self or on God.

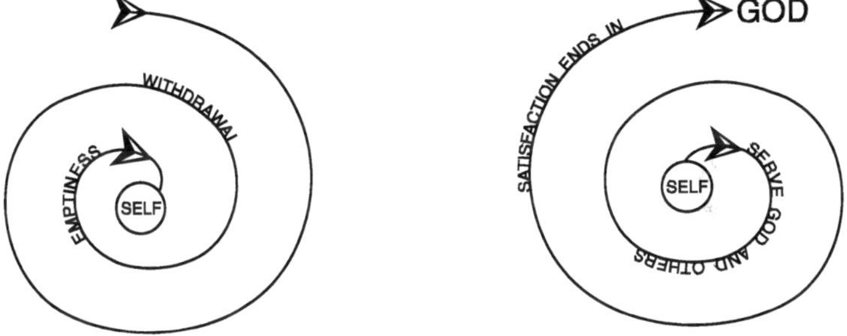

Result of Focusing on Self   Result of Focusing on God

Figure 7: Focus on Self/Focus on God

If people focus on God, they will come to be mature with respect to faith because as one focuses on God, one begins to reflect God's nature. As God is holy and righteous and has a loving and sharing nature, His people who focus on Him will begin to reflect His love and to share of themselves in loving service to others. Their lives also will begin to reflect righteousness since sin will have less and less appeal

---

[235] See Hosea 4:1-6; 6:6. God spoke to the Romans in a similar manner in Romans 1:28. Also, the Apostle Paul told the Corinthians it was a shame that some did not have the knowledge of God (1 Corinthians 15:34).

[236] Ephesians 1:17 (NIV); see also Colossians 1:9-10.

[237] Compliments of Phil Walker, Sacramento, CA.

and hold on them because where there is the light of the Lord, darkness must flee (1 John 1:5).

Focusing on God leads to maturity; it occurs through gaining knowledge and understanding of the Lord which leads to the wisdom of God. "Wisdom is connected with knowing and understanding God."[238] And wisdom and maturity are evident in sharing of oneself with others.

Analysis

The true Church was to be a mature Church according to Scripture. It was to be without spot or wrinkle, but holy and blameless (Ephesians 5:27; 2 Peter 3:14). And it was to be God's witness according to Acts 1:8 (NRSV): "You will receive power when the Holy Spirit has come upon you; and you will be my witnesses in Jerusalem, in all Judea and Samaria, and to the ends of the earth." And the Church was God's witness throughout the world as much as was possible during the scriptural time frame (Colossians 1:6). It focused on God and grew in knowledge of Him, and it w outgoing. And there were results; the Church grew and multiplied. At long last, the people of God matured in faith and had identity and real meaning to their lives. Through Christ Jesus, they became a special people used by God, a holy people reflecting the Lord's righteousness, and a priestly people, taking God's transforming message to the world.

---

[238]C. Stephen Evans, "Developing Wisdom in Christian Psychologists," Journal of Psychology and Theology, vol. 20, no. 2 (1992), 112.

PART IV

SUMMARY

The faith developmental stages set forth by James Fowler have been helpful in analyzing God's people as depicted biblically by the nation of Israel and the Church. The growth of His people was seen to fit the human developmental stages of faith as meaning making.

In considering the Old Testament nation of Israel as a son being birthed by God and then growing and developing under the guidance of a loving and patient heavenly Father, greater understanding is gained of God and His ways and what He expected from His children at each stage of their childhood development. But when they were adults, He expected more from them and gave them greater revelation through His Son, Christ Jesus. In fact, His Son was the fulfillment of the ritual and symbolism they had learned about as children. Those of God's people who grew to adulthood, metaphorically speaking, were able to perceive the greater truth that God revealed through His Son. But because many Israelites rejected God's Son, those who received him broke away from the traditional Israelite group and became known as Christians, followers of Christ. These people formed the Church.

When God's people became of age, they began to fulfill the purpose God had intended for them all along. They became His special people, to represent Him in holiness and righteousness to the world. As such, they were a distinct people with a recognized identity. And this identity provided them with meaning and purpose and significance. This identity was achieved upon maturity, because in maturity they had a secure awareness of who they were, God's people who had been redeemed, and they had hope for the future. Consequently, they were free to look outwardly, and as a result, God's people, the Church, shared the transforming love of God abroad to others (Romans 5:5) with their redeeming message of life for this world and eternity.

Thus, "Israel" came to maturity and was known as the Church. "God prevailed" indeed! And His son developed to serve Him. Amen!

SELECTED BIBLIOGRAPHY

Academic American Encyclopedia, 1993 ed. S.v. "Bruner, Jerome Seymour"; "Cognitive Psychology"; "Developmental Psychology"; "Erikson, Erik"; "Freud, Sigmund"; "Learning Theory"; "Moral Awareness"; "Personality"; "Piaget, Jean"; "Psychoanalysis"; "Psychohistory"; "Religion."

American Heritage Dictionary, The, 1986 ed. S.v. "Cognition"; "Ego"; "Faith"; "Identity"; "Maturity"; "Moral"; "Morality"; "Personality"; "Religion"; "Spiritual"; "Wisdom."

Avery, William O. "A Lutheran Examines James W. Fowler." Religious Education, vol. 85, no. 1 (Winter 1990), 69-83.

Baltes, Paul B., and K. Warner Schaie, eds. Life-Span Developmental Psychology: Personality and Socialization. New York: Academic Press, 1973.

Bandura, Albert. Social Foundations of Thought and Action: A Social Cognitive Theory. Englewood Cliffs, NJ: Prentice-Hall, Inc., 1986.

Barbeau, Clayton C. Creative Marriage: The Middle Years. New York: The Seabury Press, 1976.

Barber, Lucie W. "Are We Ready to Take Preschool Religious Education Seriously?" Religious Education, vol. 86, no. 1 (Winter 1991), 62-72.

Barnes, Albert. Barnes' Notes: Ephesians, Philippians, Colossians. Edited by Robert Frew. Grand Rapids: MI: Baker Book House, 1884-85.

Berthoud, Jean-Marc. "The Citizens' Faith." Chalcedon Report, no. 288 (July 1989), 10-11.

Birren, James E. "Spiritual Maturity in Psychological Development." Journal of Religious Gerontology, vol. 7, nos. 1/2 (1990), 41-53.

Blumfield, Michael. "Our Parents, Our Selves." The Sacramento Bee, Scene, February 27, 1993.

Brand, Paul, and Philip Yancey. In His Image. Grand Rapids: Zondervan Publishing House, 1984.

Breger, Louis. From Instinct to Identity: The Development of Personality. Englewood Cliffs, NJ: Prentice-Hall, Inc., 1974.

Bromiley, Geoffrey W., gen. ed. The International Standard Bible Encyclopedia, fully revised, vol. 2. Grand Rapids, MI: William B. Eerdmans Publishing Company, 1982. S.v. "First-Born; Firstling," by T. Lewis.

Bronfenbrenner, Urie. The Ecology of Human Development: Experiments by Nature and Design. Cambridge, MA: Harvard University Press, 1979.

Brown, Francis, S. R. Driver, Charles A. Briggs, and William Gesenius. The New Brown-Driver-Briggs-Gesenius Hebrew and English Lexicon. N.p.: Christian Copyrights, Inc., 1979.

Bruner, Jerome. Acts of Meaning. Cambridge, MA: Harvard University Press, 1990.

Buttrick, George Arthur, dict. ed. The Interpreter's Dictionary of the Bible, vol. 2. Nashville: Abingdon Press, 1962. S.v. "First-Born," by V. H. Kooy.

__________. The Interpreter's Dictionary of the Bible: An Illustrated Encyclopedia, vol. 4. Nashville, TN: Abingdon Press, 1962. S.v. "Spirit," by S. V. McCasland.

Clark, Don. "An Ancient Faith and the Modern Media." Chalcedon Report, no. 312 (July 1991), 9-10.

Clements, William M. "Spiritual Development in the Fourth Quarter of Life." Journal of Religious Gerontology, vol. 7, nos. 1/2 (1990) 55-69.

Coffey, Roberta W. "The Wisdom of Age." The Sacramento Bee, 14 January 1993, Scene 1, 5.

Concise Columbia Encyclopedia, 1989 ed. S.v. "Erikson, Erik"; "Freud, Sigmund"; "Piaget, Jean"; "Psychoanalysis"; "Religion."

Douglas, J. D., org. ed. New Bible Dictionary, 2nd ed. Wheaton: Tyndale House Publishers, Inc., 1982. S.v. "First-Born," by M. J. Selman; s.v. "Synagogue," by C. L. Feinberg.

Drovdahl, Robert R., and Les L. Steele. "Identity Formation and College-Level Religion Courses: A Pilot Study." Journal of Psychology and Theology, vol. 19, no. 2 (1991), 197-202.

Duska, Ronald, and Mariellen Whelan. Moral Development: A Guide to Piaget and Kohlberg. New York: Paulist press, 1975.

Elwell, Walter A., Editor. Evangelical Dictionary of Theology. Grand Rapids, MI: Baker Book House, 1984. S.v. "Spirit."

Erikson, Erik. The Life Cycle Completed. New York: W. W. Norton & Company, 1982.

__________. The Life Cycle Completed: A Review. New York: W. W. Norton & Company, 1982.

Evans, C. Stephen. "Developing Wisdom in Christian Psychologists." Journal of Psychology and Theology, vol. 20, no. 2 (1992), 110-118.

Ford-Grabowsky, Mary. "Flaws in Faith-Development Theory." Religious Education, vol. 82, no. 1 (Winter 1987), 80-93.

Foulkes, Francis. Tyndale New Testament Commentaries: Ephesians, vol. 10. Revised ed. Grand Rapids, MI: William B. Eerdmans Publishing Company, 1989.

Fowler, James W. Stages of Faith: The Psychology of Human Development and the Quest for Meaning. San Francisco: HarperCollins, Publishers, 1981.

__________. "The Enlightenment and Faith Development Theory." Journal of Empirical Theology, vol. 1, no. 1 (1988), 29-42.

Fowlkes, Mary Ann. "Roots of Ritual in Social Interactive Episodes During the First Three Years of Life: Implications for Bonding in the Faith Community." Religious Education, vol. 84, no. 3 (Summer 1989), 338-348.

Gæbelein, Frank E. The Expositor's Bible Commentary, vol. 3. Grand Rapids, MI: Zondervan Publishing House, 1992.

Green, Charles W., and Cindy L. Hoffman. "Stages of Faith and Perceptions of Similar and Dissimilar Others." Review of Religious Research, vol. 30, no. 3 (March 1989), 246-254.

Grimley, Liam K. "A Theological Perspective of Kohlberg's Sixth Stage of Moral Development." Journal of Psychology and Christianity, vol. 10, no. 4 (Winter 1991), 293-299.

Grossman, Barbara A. "Faith and Personal Development: A Renewed Link for Judaism." Journal of Psychology and Judaism, vol. 16, no. 1 (Spring 1992), 19-29.

Guthrie, Donald. <u>Tyndale New Testament Commentaries: Hebrews</u>, vol. 15. Grand Rapids, MI: William B. Eerdmans Publishing Company, 1983.

Hagner, Donald A. <u>New International Biblical Commentary: Hebrews</u>, vol. 14. Peabody, MA: Hendrickson Publishers, 1990.

Hall, Christopher A. "Holy Health." <u>Christianity Today</u>, vol. 36, no. 14 (November 23, 1992), 19-22.

Halverson, Delia. "Faith-Building Lifestyles: Enabling Teachers and Parents to Share Their Faith with Children and Youth." <u>Religious Education</u>, vol. 83, no. 4 (Fall 1988), 526-530.

Hanford, Jack T. "The Relationship Between Faith Development of James Fowler and Moral Development of Lawrence Kohlberg: A Theoretical Review." <u>Journal of Psychology and Christianity</u>, vol. 10, no. 4 (Winter 1991), 306-310.

<u>Holy Bible: New International Version</u>. Grand Rapids, MI: Zondervan Bible Publishers, 1984.

<u>Holy Bible: New Revised Standard Version with Apocrypha</u>. New York: Oxford University Press, 1989.

Huebner, Dwayne. "Christian Growth in Faith." <u>Religious Education</u>, vol. 81, no. 4 (Fall 1986), 511-521.

Ingram, Jay. <u>Twins</u>. New York: Simon and Schuster, Inc., 1988.

Jardine, Marlene M., and Henning G. Viljoen. "Fowler's Theory of Faith Development: An Evaluative Discussion." <u>Religious Education</u>, vol. 87, no. 1 (Winter 1992), 74-85.

Jones, Stanton L. Jones, Elizabeth J. Watson, and Timothy J. Wolfram. "Results of the Rech Conference Survey on Religious Faith and Professional Psychology." <u>Journal of Psychology and Theology</u>, vol. 20, no. 2 (1992), 147-158.

Jones, Jessie Orton. <u>Secrets</u>. New York: The Viking Press, 1945.

Kay Cassill. <u>Twins: Natures Amazing Mystery</u>. New York: Atheneum, 1982.

Kimble, Melvin A. "Aging and the Search for Meaning." <u>Journal of Religious Gerontology</u>, vol. 7, nos. 1/2 (1990), 111-127.

King, Robert H. "Review of <u>Faith on Earth: An Inquiry into the Structure of Human Faith</u>, by H. Richard Niebuhr." <u>Religious Studies Review</u>, vol. 17, no. 4 (October 1991), 293-295.

Kohlberg, Lawrence. <u>Essays on Moral Development</u>. Vol. 1, <u>The Philosophy of Moral Development: Moral Stages and the Idea of Justice</u>. San Francisco: Harper & Row, Publishers, 1981.

Lane, William L. <u>Hebrews: A Call to Commitment</u>. Peabody, MA: Hendrickson Publishers, 1985.

LaRossa, Ralph, and Maureen Mulligan LaRossa. <u>Transition to Parenthood: How Infants Change Families</u>. Beverly Hills, CA: Sage Publications, 1981.

LeVine, Robert A. <u>Culture, Behavior, and Personality: An Introduction to the Comparative Study of Psychosocial Adaptation</u>. New York: Aldine Publishing Company, 1982.

Lewin, Kurt. <u>A Dynamic Theory of Personality: Selected Papers</u>. Translated by Donald K. Adams and Karl E. Zenner. New York: McGraw-Hill Book Company, Inc., 1935.

Lockyer, Herbert, Sr., gen. ed. <u>Nelson's Illustrated Bible Dictionary</u>. Nashville: Thomas Nelson Publishers, 1986. S.v. "Firstborn."

Logos Bible Software, version 1.6b. King James Version, New King James Version, New International Version, New Revised Standard Version. Oak Harbor, WA: Logos Research Systems, Inc., 1993.

MacArthur, John, Jr. "Faith According to the Apostle James." Journal of the Evangelical Theological Society, vol. 33, no. 1 (March 1990), 13-34.

Malony, H. Newton, and Donald D. Hoagland. "Moral Development: A Review of Empirical Research." Religious Studies Review, vol. 10, no. 4 (October 1984), 343-347.

Maslow Abraham H. Toward a Psychology of Being. 2nd ed. Princeton, NJ: D. Van Nostrand Company, Inc., 1968.

Mason, David R. "Faith, Religion, and Theology." Journal of Religious Studies, vol. 15, nos. 1 & 2 (1989), 1-15.

McDargh, John. "Faith-Development Theory at Ten Years." Religious Studies Review, vol. 10, no. 4 (October 1984), 339-342.

Milbank, Dana. "What's in a Name?" Reader's Digest (March 1993): 145-146. Quoted from The Wall Street Journal (September 21, 1992).

Moberg, David O. "Spiritual Maturity and Wholeness in the Later Years." Journal of Religious Gerontology, vol. 7, nos. 1/2 (1990), 5-24.

Morris, Henry M. The Biblical Basis for Modern Science. Grand Rapids, MI: Baker Book House, 1984.

Moseley, Romney M. "Forms of Logic in Faith Development Theory." Pastoral Psychology, vol. 39, no. 3 (January 1991), 143-152.

Myers, David G. "Who's Happy? Who's Not?" Christianity Today, vol. 36, no. 14 (November 23, 1992), 23-26.

Narramore, Bruce. "Barriers to the Integration of Faith and Learning in Christian Graduate Training Programs in Psychology." Journal of Psychology and Theology, vol. 20, no. 2 (1992), 119-126.

Nelson's Illustrated Bible Dictionary, 1986 ed. S.v. "Name."

New Bible Dictionary: Second Edition, 1982. S.v. "Name."

Osmer, Richard R. "Faith Development in the Adult Life Cycle: A Review." Religious Education, vol. 84, no. 4 (Fall 1989), 483-493.

________. "James W. Fowler and the Reformed Tradition: An Exercise in Theological Reflection in Religious Education." Religious Education, vol. 85, no. 1 (Winter 1990), 51-68.

Parks, Sharon. "Young Adult Faith Development: Teaching Is the Context of Theological Education." Religious Education, vol. 77, no. 6 (November-December 1982), 657-672.

Patzia, Arthur G. New International Biblical Commentary: Epehsians, Colossians, Philemon,. vol. 10. Peabody, MA: Hendrickson Publishers, 1990.

Payne, Barbara. "Spiritual Maturity and Meaning-Filled Relationships: A Sociological Perspective." Journal of Religious Gerontology, vol. 7, nos. 1/2 (1990), 25-39.

Radmacher, Earl D. "First Response to 'Faith According to the Apostle James' by John F. MacArthur, Jr." Journal of the Evangelical Theological Society, vol. 33, no. 1 (March 1990), 35-41.

Rainbow, Jon. "Spiritual and Faith Development in the Later Years." The Journal of the Faculty of the Southern Baptist Theological Seminary, vol. 88, no. 3 (Summer 1991), 195-204.

Ratcliff, Donald. "Baby Faith: Infants, Toddlers, and Religion." Religious Education, vol. 87, no. 1 (Winter 1992), 117-126.

Reader's Digest, "Personal Glimpses: Wildfire," (April 1993).

Reader's Digest Great Encyclopedic Dictionary, The, 1975 ed. S.v. "Dictionary of Quotations"; "Masculine Names"; "Wisdom."

Ripple, Richard, Robert F. Biehler, and Gail A. Jaquish. Human Development. Boston: Houghton Mifflin Company, 1982.

Rohm, Robert A. Positive Personality Insights. Columbus, GA: Brentwood Christian Press, 1992.

Rushdoony, Mark R. "Faith, Law & Christ." Chalcedon Report, no. 308 (March 1991), 7-8.

________. "The Obedience of Faith: Romans 16." Chalcedon Report, no. 328 (November 1992), 4-5.

Rushdoony, Rousas John. "Reality, Faith, and Architecture." Chalcedon Report, no. 293 (December 1989), 16-17.

Santoli, Al, "I Like You Just The Way You Are," *Parade Magazine*, The Sacramento Bee, (March 28, 1993), 4-5.

Saucy, Robert L. "Second Response to 'Faith According to the Apostle James' by John F. MacArthur, Jr." Journal of the Evangelical Theological Society, vol. 33, no. 1 (March 1990), 35-41.

Seeber, James J. "Spiritual Maturity and Wholeness—A Concept Whose Time Has Come." Journal of Religious Gerontology, vol. 7, nos. 1/2 (1990), 1-3.

Stokes, Kenneth. "Faith Development in the Adult Life Cycle." Journal of Religious Gerontology, vol. 7, nos. 1/2 (1990), 167-184.

Sugarman, Leonie. Life-Span Development: Concepts, Theories and Interventions. New York: Methuen and Company, Limited, 1986.

Tenney, Merrill C., gen. ed. The Zondervan Pictorial Encyclopedia of the Bible, vol. 2. Grand Rapids, MI: Zondervan Publishing Company, 1976. S.v. "First-Born," by J.E. Rosscup.

________. The Zondervan Pictorial Encyclopedia of the Bible, vol. 5. Grand Rapids, MI: Zondervan Publishing House, 1976. S.v. "Spirit," by F. Foulkes.

Thiessen, Henry C. Lectures in Systematic Theology. Revised by Vernon D. Doerksen. Grand Rapids, MI: William B. Eerdmans Publishing Company, 1979.

Torrance, Thomas F. The Mediation of Christ. Grand Rapids, MI: William B. Eerdmans Publishing Company, 1983.

Welch, Claude. "Review of Faith on Earth: An Inquiry into the Structure of Human Faith, by H. Richard Niebuhr." Religious Studies Review, vol. 17, no. 4 (October 1991), 289-293.

Widmann, Ruth Dunn. "'Lost in the Immensity of God': A Pre-Civil War Methodist Woman's Experience of the Presence and Power of God." Methodist History, vol. XXV, no. 3 (April 1987), 164-175.

Wilder-Smith, A. E. "The Origin of Conceptual Thought in Living Systems." Impact: Vital Articles on Science/ Creation, no. 236 (February 1993).

Williams, Gurney III. Twins. New York: Franklin Watts, 1979.

Wilson, Marvin R. Our Father Abraham: Jewish Roots of the Christian Faith. Grand Rapids: William B. Eerdmans Publishing Company, 1989.

Wink, Walter. "The Education of the Apostles: Mark's View of Human Transformation." Religious Education, vol. 83, no. 2 (Spring 1988), 277-290.

Yates, David O. What the Bible Says About Your Personality. San Francisco: Harper & Row, Publishers, 1980.

Biblical Education for Busy Learners

Bible and Spiritual Enrichment
Education for Ministerial Credentials
College Degrees – Experiential Learning

– Non-Denominational –
Options of Online Streaming Audio, Audio CDs or Tapes
Affordable, High-Quality Education and Training

Come enjoy the
~ FRAGRANCE / "REYAH" ~
of the knowledge of Christ

*"Thanks be to God, who always leads us in triumphal procession in Christ
and through us spreads everywhere the fragrance of the knowledge of him."*
2 Corinthians 2:14

916/924-1919

PO Box 1207, Citrus Heights, CA 95611

www.Reyah.org   Contact@Reyah.org   www.Reyah.org

NOTICE OF NONDISCRIMINATORY POLICY AS TO STUDENTS

The Reyah Group admits students of any race, color, national, and ethnic origin to all the rights,
privileges, programs and activities generally accorded or made available to students at the
school. It does not discriminate on the basis of race, color, national, and ethnic origin in
administration of educational policies, admissions policies, scholarship and loan programs, and
athletic and other school-administered programs.